TALES OF
ANCIENT WORLDS

NEON SQUID

CONTENTS

WELCOME TO THE ANCIENT WORLD

There's nothing I like better than exploring the ancient past. Our history is a never-ending fountain of incredible tales, brilliant adventures, and fantastic people. I've been obsessed with archaeology ever since I was your age, exploring my town and discovering its history. I believe that when we understand our past, we understand ourselves a little better, too. It can help us appreciate the beautiful world that we live in.

But what is archaeology? Archaeology is the study of all of the physical things humans leave behind as they go through life. Our houses, our bones and teeth, even the stuff we flush down the toilet. It's all archaeology! As we go through life we leave these little bits behind, sprinkling little clues all over the Earth, almost like pieces of a puzzle.

Archaeologists use the most advanced scientific tools available (and some shovels and trowels) to give us insights into the lives of our ancestors. Radar that can scan the ground, lasers that can tell us the age of artefacts, and drones that whizz above the desert – it's all like something out of a science fiction movie.

In this book we're going to take a look at how archaeologists have used these tools to put together the pieces of our jigsaw puzzle. We're going to explore the entire Earth, travelling back in time millions of years to our earliest ancestors. We'll recreate the lives of ancient kings and queens (plus a grumpy merchant). We'll explore ancient cities that sank beneath the waves or were swallowed by dense jungle, and we'll travel the oceans with intrepid explorers. Along the way, expect some funky gods, mind-blowing treasures, and grisly warriors.

Are you ready for an adventure? Are you ready to unearth some tales of the ancient world?

Stefan

CHAPTER ONE
THE FIRST HUMANS

The oldest adventures in archaeology are very old indeed. We're not talking about thousands of years, but millions! Let's begin by exploring the earliest chapter in human history – the Stone Age. We'll start over three million years ago with a bunch of hairy upright-walking apes. Then we'll meet modern globe-trotting humans, before ending up around 6,000 years ago with the first farmers and their majestic monuments, including the gobsmacking Göbekli Tepe and the stunning Stonehenge.

YOUR ANCIENT
FAMILY TREE

It's only right to start this book with the most ancient tale of all, the story of humanity! You may look very similar to your mum and dad, but not *exactly* the same. Over time small differences like this add up, and animals very slowly change into something entirely new. This is called evolution. Over the last 7 million years we evolved from apes in Africa, like chimpanzees, into modern humans.

Sahelanthropus

These apes lived around 7 million years ago and may be one of our first ancestors to start walking on two legs – at least some of the time. We can tell this because of how their necks connected to their heads. Walking on two legs is one of the defining features of humans, and a good sign an animal is our ancestor. All other apes mostly walk on all fours.

Early tools

Australopithecus

Evolving around 3.5 million years ago, Australopithecus lived all across East Africa. They walked on two legs, but their brains were only slightly bigger than a chimpanzee's. Despite this, Australopithecus was probably the first of our ancestors to use stone tools!

Paranthropus boisei

Paranthropus evolved 2.6 million years ago. They aren't our direct ancestor, more like a cousin. They walked on two legs but ate a diet that consisted mostly of leaves and grasses. Almost like human cows. They had big teeth – a result of all that chewing!

Neanderthal

Neanderthals were very similar to us, just shorter and stockier. This was because they evolved in Europe around 400,000 years ago, where the climate was much colder than Africa (where modern humans evolved). Their bulky bodies helped them conserve heat.

Homo erectus

Our ancestors really started to look like us 1.9 million years ago. Homo erectus had hairless bodies, and could run on two feet, making them good hunters. They had brains almost as big as ours and were able to leave Africa and spread across Asia.

Homo erectus made their own handaxes.

Homo sapiens

Our species, Homo sapiens, evolved in Africa around 300,000 years ago. We owe so much to our ancient ancestors, but we have bigger brains – we're the nerds of our family tree! Our big brains allowed us to be creative, adapt to anything, and produce incredible tools and art.

THE STORY OF A GIRL CALLED LUCY

Donald Johanson and Tom Gray had been working in the hot sun all morning, surveying the land around Hadar, in the East African country of Ethiopia. It was 1974 and they were searching for tiny clues of our **earliest ancestors** – relatives of ours that lived millions of years ago. They weren't having much joy so decided to head back to their car and try a different route.

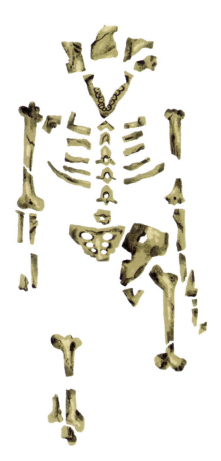

As they were walking back they noticed a bone sticking out of the ground. They excitedly began clearing away dirt – revealing part of a skull! After two weeks of work they had stumbled upon one of the most incredible discoveries in the history of science, an almost complete **Australopithecus**, which they decided to name Lucy (after a song by the Beatles).

Australopithecus was one of our earliest relatives. In many ways it was more similar to a chimpanzee than to a modern human. It was small, hairy, and probably spent some of the time living in trees. If you were alive 3 million years ago, you'd be short and hairy too.

Lucy had big teeth. She didn't know how to make a fire, so everything she ate was raw. Naturally when your diet is made up of tough bits of food you need **big gnashers** to chew through it all.

How do we know this pile of bones was your great-great-great-great (x 100,000) grandma? It's all down to the legs and hips. Different animals walk in different ways: your legs are not the same as a cat's legs, and a cat's legs aren't the same as a mouse's. Lucy was definitely designed to walk upright on two legs, and her feet were shaped like ours. She didn't walk or run as well as you though, but had a **funny waddle**. The fact that she couldn't run very fast probably means she wasn't a great hunter. If Lucy ate any (raw) meat, it was likely because she had found an old dead animal. Tasty!

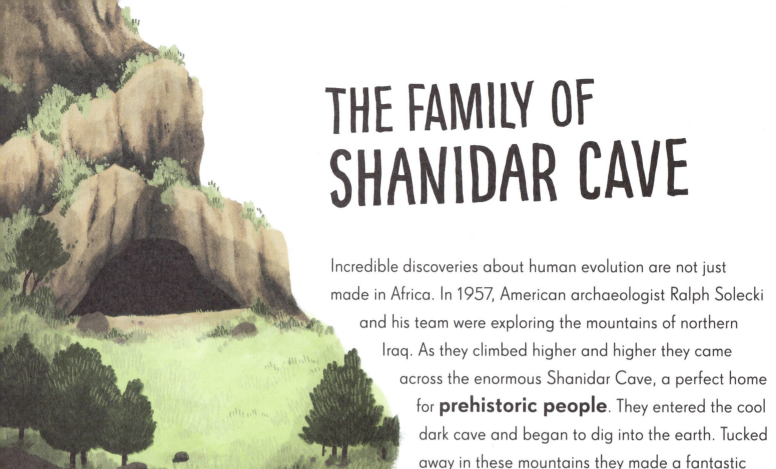

THE FAMILY OF SHANIDAR CAVE

Incredible discoveries about human evolution are not just made in Africa. In 1957, American archaeologist Ralph Solecki and his team were exploring the mountains of northern Iraq. As they climbed higher and higher they came across the enormous Shanidar Cave, a perfect home for **prehistoric people**. They entered the cool dark cave and began to dig into the earth. Tucked away in these mountains they made a fantastic discovery – bones and stone tools left behind by a group of Neanderthals 50,000 years ago!

The Neanderthals were our closest cousins. In many ways they looked and acted like us. They lived in caves, hunted wild animals, buried their dead, and even made small pieces of artwork. They had slightly different skulls from us, and they were a little shorter and wider. Imagine a family of **professional wrestlers** and you're along the right lines.

As skeleton after skeleton was recovered from Shanidar Cave more evidence emerged of how similar Neanderthals were to us. The best example came from the skull of a male Neanderthal called Shanidar 1. When Shanidar 1 was young he was hit on the head really badly. Not a little bump, but a life-threatening injury that caused terrible damage.

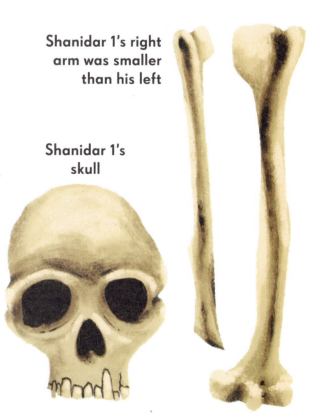

Shanidar 1's right arm was smaller than his left

Shanidar 1's skull

Shanidar 1 was probably **blind and deaf** on the injured side of his head. The wound also caused his arm and leg to not grow properly. For someone who had to hunt for a living, you would think that should spell disaster, but it wasn't the case.

As it turned out, Shanidar 1 lived until he was about 45 years old. Not too bad for a caveman! This meant that Shanidar 1 was probably helped by other Neanderthals, most likely his family, and must have had a respected role in their group.

This was a really important discovery. Previously it was thought that Neanderthals led a hard, uncaring life. Now we know they loved and cared for their family, just like us.

THE BABY THAT LOVED TO CLIMB

In 2000, Zeresenay Alemseged and his team were excavating in the Dikika region of Ethiopia, part of an area called the **Great Rift Valley**. The region is hot and dry, but it's a great place to study ancient humans. As the team sifted through the dust, bucket after bucket, searching for any clue, they uncovered a small, cute, and incredibly important fossil: the 3.3-million-year-old remains of a 3-year-old Australopithecus! (Try saying that quickly.)

Zeresenay knew this was a special discovery. It's incredibly rare to find bones that are over 3 million years old, but it's even harder to find the remains of children because their bones are fragile and less likely to fossilise.

Zeresenay called the child **"Lucy's baby"** in honour of the other famous Australopith discovery (see pages 10–11). Scientists got to work studying the remains. Even though the child was very young it was clear that it was able to walk upright, just like us. Lucy's baby probably held its mother's hand as they wandered across the hot savannah.

The finger and toe bones were curved, similar to modern chimpanzees and gorillas. Modern apes have these features to help them climb trees. This suggests that Lucy's baby was doing the same thing.

Why would an animal that walked on two legs also need to be good at climbing? We don't know for sure, but we can make some educated guesses. Life in the African savannah can be very dangerous. The area is full of lions, hyenas, and cheetahs, animals that would absolutely **love to eat you for breakfast**. Australopiths like Lucy's baby might have climbed into trees at night to keep them safe from predators. You don't want to wake up in the morning and discover a hyena licking your feet!

Lucy's baby is a great example of how slowly humans adapted, or evolved, over millions of years. Even though they walked on two legs like modern humans, Australopiths still had many similarities to other apes. Even to this day, we still find it fun to climb – maybe that's the ape inside of you!

THE SKULL OF JEBEL IRHOUD

Western Morocco is a hot and dry region of Africa. On the side of a dusty rock face, just outside Jebel Irhoud, Jean-Jacques Hublin, Abdelouahed Ben-Ncer, and their team were searching for clues to humanity's origins.

At first glance it would seem like a pointless task. Most of the major finds in human evolution came from eastern and southern Africa, not all the way in the northwest. What they were about to find would change our understanding of human evolution forever. As they dug down, they found the most important artefact any human can ever leave behind, their skull. As our **big brains** are the most defining feature of Homo sapiens, we can tell so much from finding human skulls.

Stone tools were also found at the site.

One big debate in prehistory is when our modern brains emerged. Did they evolve quickly, or very slowly over hundreds of thousands of years? This skull from Jebel Irhoud is a key piece of the puzzle, maybe the most important piece found so far.

The skull

Even though the skull is not quite as round as a modern human's, it is very, very similar. Much more like ours than any of our evolutionary cousins, like **Neanderthals**. A Neanderthal skull was shaped like a rugby ball, and very thick-boned. The skull from Jebel Irhoud was rounder and had delicate cheeks, just like you.

The skull was dated to around **300,000 years ago**. This was truly an incredible discovery. It was the oldest Homo sapiens skull ever found, by over 100,000 years! This tells us two important things. Firstly, our modern features evolved over a longer period of time than we thought. Secondly, our evolution occurred all over Africa, it wasn't just confined to the south and east as we previously thought.

It seems it took us quite a while to leave Africa and spread around the world. Jebel Irhoud is 120,000 years older than the earliest Homo sapiens found outside of Africa, which was in Israel. Although who knows what future archaeologists might find!

The possible routes Homo sapiens took out of Africa

THE SECRET HISTORY OF MADJEDBEBE

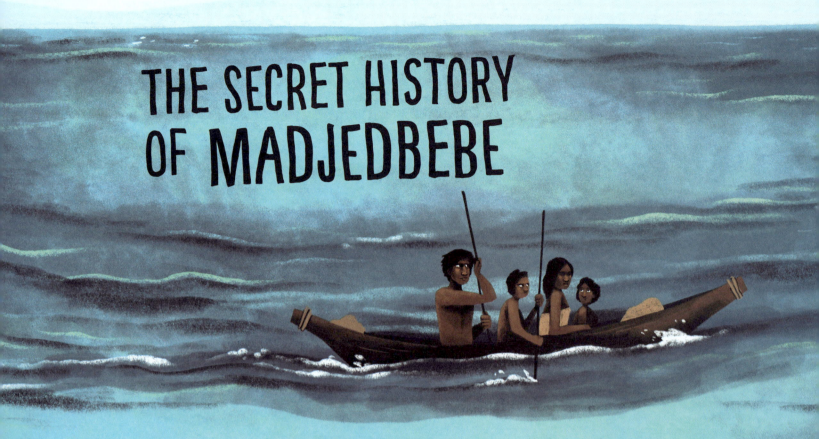

Chris Clarkson had been digging in Australia's far north for weeks, swatting away the mosquitoes trying to bite him. Above him towered a cliff covered in **Aboriginal artwork**, a visual history of the people that have lived in the area for thousands of years. However, Chris was about to make a discovery that would push that history even further back in time.

As Chris and his team were digging they found tools, an axe head, grindstones, and a fireplace surrounded by flaked stones. The finds kept on coming – eventually they discovered the ancient remains of 17 humans.

The archaeologists had made a deal with the **Mirarr**, the traditional owners of Madjedbebe, which allowed them to study any artefacts they found, as long as they buried them again when the work was done. This was important to the Mirarr, who feel a strong connection to the remains of their ancestors. The team of archaeologists then used an incredible scientific technique. They shone a special light at the artefacts they'd unearthed, allowing them to calculate when the objects had been buried.

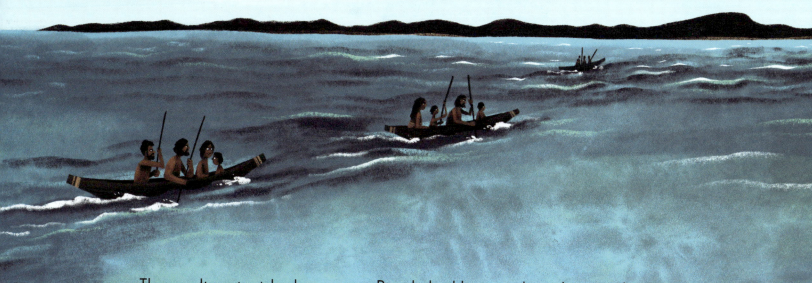

The results astonished everyone. People had been making these tools, grinding vegetables, and sitting around the fires **65,000 years ago!** This was the earliest ever evidence of humans in Australia.

When humans arrived in Australia is an important question for archaeologists. Sixty-five thousand years ago sea levels were lower than they are now, and Australia was connected to Papua New Guinea to the north, forming an area we call Sahul. However, Australia has always been separated from mainland Asia, which means that to get there humans had to use boats.

To be able to sail across the water with your family and friends would not have been easy. Your canoe could capsize, you could be blown off course, or a storm could toss you into the water. To make the journey required determination and adaptability, skills that would help Aboriginal people in their exploration of Australia. If it wasn't for the Mirarr and Chris Clarkson, we wouldn't know just how long ago such a feat was achieved.

Possible route

Sahul

Madjedbebe

WELCOME TO THE AMERICAS

Twenty-five thousand years ago, virtually all of Canada and Alaska was frozen, cutting the Americas off from the rest of the world. Isolated from the humans that were busy making rhino stew across Europe and Asia, huge beasts were able to evolve. One of the most bizarre was the **glyptodon**, a grass-munching beast the size of a car, protected by thick armour and a spiky tail. Basically it was like a cow, crossed with a tank, crossed with a Stegosaurus.

However, even the glyptodons' mighty armour couldn't protect them from what was to come. At some point, humans crossed into North America using a land bridge that connected it to Asia. As there was so much ice, they probably moved along the coast, going from beach to beach in small canoes. The Pacific coast of the Americas is lined with **kelp forests**. These huge fields of giant seaweed support lots of wildlife and could have provided the early travellers with plenty of fish on their way south.

A few thousand years later, Dr Karina Chichkoyan and her colleagues were analysing glyptodon remains from different museums (sadly no glyptodons are alive today). The team found clear scratch marks on the glyptodon bones – evidence that humans had hunted them and then carved the meat.

So when did humans arrive in the Americas? It's hard to say for sure and it is one of the most debated topics in archaeology. We know humans reached **Monte Verde** in the south of Chile at least 14,600 years ago. So they must have entered across Alaska at least a couple of thousand years before that, maybe even 10,000 years before. More evidence is needed before we can solve the puzzle.

LIFE DURING
THE ICE AGE

The world was very different 25,000 years ago. Huge glaciers, miles high, covered the north, while vast beasts roamed the earth – from enormous hairy mammoths to prides of cave-dwelling lions. Meanwhile, humans lived in small groups, spending their days following these animals across the grassy plains, ice, and snow.

Horse

Reindeer

Cave lion

Woolly rhino

Prehistoric beasts

Ice Age animals were typically bigger and hairier than animals today. This was to keep them warm in the freezing conditions. Famous animals from this period include woolly mammoths, woolly rhinos, reindeer, and horses.

Woolly mammoth

Ancient masterpieces

Life in the Ice Age was not all snowball fights and mammoth burgers. Just like people today, prehistoric people were fantastic artists. Beautiful paintings of lions hunting have been found on cave walls in France. Cave people also played music. Archaeologists have found ancient flutes made from birds' bones!

Bone flute

Wall art from Chauvet Cave in France

Crafting weapons

In the chilly Ice Age world of our ancestors, hunting weapons were essential for survival. No spears = no food. Prehistoric people created weapons out of antlers and flint, polishing them into razor-sharp, lethal tools.

THE TEMPLE OF BONES

Kostenki

Deep in the forests of southern Russia, in amongst the birch trees, sits Kostenki. Now it is surrounded by farms and winding rivers, but 25,000 years ago, during the Ice Age, it was on the edge of a frozen land. An almost never-ending sea of grass stretched from Europe across to Asia. There were few trees and little shelter from the bitingly cold wind. To live here, you had to be clever and use everything you could find in order to survive.

In 2014, archaeologists made an incredible discovery. Hidden behind a museum, underneath a small wood, lay an **enormous prehistoric building**. However it wasn't its size that was the truly remarkable thing about it, but what it was made of. This building wasn't constructed of wood, or even stone. It was built of mammoth bones!

The remains of the huge structure were 12.5 m (40 ft) across and made of the bones of at least 60 mammoths! To keep the snow and cold wind out, the outside would have been covered in mammoth skin and shaggy fur. Kind of like a tent you would go camping in (but it probably smelt a lot worse).

To build this mammoth tent the prehistoric builders first needed to hunt a mammoth. This was a **difficult and perilous job**. These animals weighed as much as three cars each and could easily hurt you with their tusks or trunks. Archaeologists can tell from the marks left on the bones that many people were involved with hunting these gargantuan beasts. This wasn't a one-person job, but an event that the whole village took part in. Even with a big team ready and raring to go, prehistoric people needed to be crafty. Sometimes they would dig big pits and ambush the animals to prevent them from escaping. You might think that it would be a horrible thing to hunt and kill such an animal, but you need to remember that in the ancient past people had no choice – they needed to eat. To go to such dangerous lengths to create the mammoth structure left the archaeologists with a burning question: what was it used for?

Typically we imagine people who lived in the Ice Age as **cave people**. However, it's not always easy to find a nice warm cave to live in. If you lived in a field out in the open, you needed to find some other way to stay warm and dry. So maybe this was a big house? As the archaeologists searched the site, more clues started appearing as to what it was used for.

Traces of ancient fires were found inside the building. Archaeologists love finding fires because we can use them to learn so much about the past. Perhaps the structure was used as the room where the village people gathered to cook and prepare the mammoths they had just hunted? The team investigating even found the burnt remains of 20,000 year old vegetables. It just shows – even if you're a big tough, Ice Age hunter, you still have to eat your greens!

People in ancient times didn't have fridges to store their food. So they would often hang meat up over a fire and the smoke would keep it from turning gross. It's possible this large building at Kostenki was a place for them to do this. One final option that can't be ruled out is that it was a **huge mammoth temple**. Archaeologists found smaller mammoth buildings around it, which were probably houses. This larger building could have been a place where these ancient hunters practised mysterious rituals. Maybe praying for a successful hunt, warm weather, or thanking the mammoths for the food they provide.

Trying to work out why people did things in prehistory is really hard. They could have been sleeping in the building, praying, eating, making mammoth bacon – or all of the above. Trying to answer these questions is what makes archaeology so exciting!

THE FARMERS OF
THE NEOLITHIC

Eleven thousand years ago, Earth's climate became warmer. At the same time, human society underwent one of the greatest technological shifts in our entire history, with the arrival of farming. I know what you're thinking: "FARMING!?" But you'll see – farming changed society forever! Archaeologists call this period the Neolithic.

Sedentism

Developing farming meant people didn't have to follow herds of animals all year any more, but could settle in one place. This is called "sedentism". Now we were able to spend our time developing new inventions.

Yayoi Japan

In Japan, the Neolithic is called the Yayoi period. People lived in large fortified villages. Their main crop was rice – harvesting it was back-breaking work for the whole village!

All over the world

Farming started in different places (the red bits on the map) at different times. Across the world, from the mountains of Peru to the fertile river valleys of Asia, people began working the earth. The warm, stable climate allowed people to grow the same crops year after year.

Crops

Without the Neolithic humans wouldn't farm wheat, potatoes, rice, or tomatoes. To put that another way – no wheat or tomatoes means no pizza!

First livestock

Why spend all day hunting, when you can just keep animals next to your house? Pigs, cows, chickens, sheep, and goats all started to be farmed in the Neolithic.

Amazing pottery

Pottery often appears alongside the development of farming. Although we take plates and cups for granted now, back then they were life-changing. Humans used pottery for cooking, eating, storage, and producing new goods like alcohol.

Village life

One big advantage of farming is that you can produce more food than you need and store it for later. This meant families got bigger, and stayed in the same place. It was important to protect your crops! This led to the first villages appearing in the archaeological record (and probably the first nosy neighbours, too).

THE VILLAGE ON THE MISTY MOUNTAIN

In 2019, Ben Shaw and his team of Australian and Papua New Guinean archaeologists were working in an extremely remote part of the world. Literally on top of a mountain, in the heart of Papua New Guinea's dense rainforest. They were searching for **ancient Neolithic villages**. It had been known for a few years that agriculture in Papua New Guinea started around 10,000 years ago. Just as farming sprang up around the rest of the world, the ancient inhabitants of Papua New Guinea started experimenting with farming yams and nuts.

However, many of the other achievements of the Neolithic – like permanent villages, sophisticated stone tools, and textiles – had never been found. Was Papua New Guinea really so different to the rest of the world, or were archaeologists looking in the wrong place? Well at Waim, on top of the mountain, they found their answer: in this most remote of places, they found the remains of a 5,000-year-old Neolithic village!

It was full of incredible discoveries. The first were holes in the ground left by ancient wooden beams. This showed that the farmers here were constructing solid buildings, which meant they were staying in one place for a long time. They found stone axes and tools made from obsidian (obsidian is a super sharp rock made when volcanoes explode – it's even sharper than a surgical scalpel!). This obsidian had come all the way from **New Britain**, an island to the east of Papua New Guinea. This shows that the villagers had extensive trade networks!

Carved face

The team found red rocks, called ochre, that were probably used to dye fabrics. And finally, a brilliant carved stone face. Another perfect example of the creativity that was unleashed once humans had developed farming. There's something so special about finding a carving of a face, there are so many questions that spring to mind. Who were they? Was it a self-portrait? Was it someone the artist loved? Was it their child? Was it their god?

The discoveries at Waim have completely rewritten our understanding of Neolithic Papua New Guinea.

THE TOWER OF JERICHO

The town of Jericho sits on a small hill overlooking the Jordan River in Palestine. This small hill is not natural, though. It wasn't made by any earthquakes, or volcanoes, or anything like that. It is what archaeologists call a **"tell"**. As a result of people living in the same place for thousands of years the town has literally been lifted up, as each generation built on top of the last. This has created a small hill full to the brim with archaeology! At the bottom of Jericho's tell was a particularly incredible find – one of the oldest buildings in the entire world.

In 1952, British archaeologist **Kathleen Kenyon** and her team of local experts were excavating along an old city wall deep inside the tell. Before Kathleen excavated, archaeologists thought these walls dated to around 1000 BCE. As Kathleen made her way along the wall she uncovered evidence that it was much, much older than that. The town dated back to the very earliest days of the Neolithic, around **8000** BCE. This meant Jericho was probably the oldest town that has been continuously inhabited in the world!

Kathleen continued to excavate the wall when she made a jaw-dropping discovery: a huge ancient tower. Archaeologists have long debated what it was used for. Some wondered if it was used to store grain, but it turned out the tower was solid, with just one small staircase rising through the middle.

Perhaps it was used as a point to observe the setting Sun? The tower is aligned with the nearby Quruntul mountain and in the middle of summer, known as the **summer solstice**, the Sun sets at the same position over the tower and the mountain. Perhaps Neolithic folks gathered here with their friends and family to watch the sun set on a glorious summer's day!

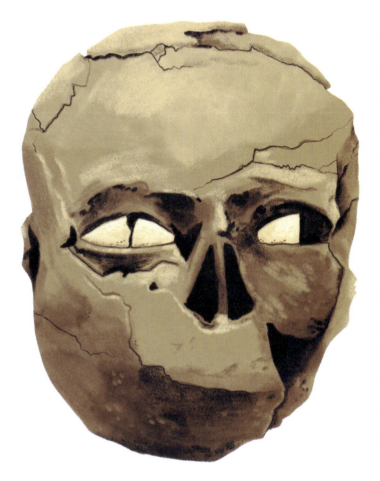

The great tower of Jericho was not the only fantastic discovery made by Kathleen. One day her team were digging in the remains of a Neolithic building when they unearthed something much more grisly. **Peter Parr**, one of Kathleen's students, moved a rock. Underneath lay not just one human skull, but seven!

Skulls can be quite common in archaeological sites, but there was something really special about these ones. They weren't buried with their bodies and, fascinatingly, they were decorated! Each of the skulls was covered in plaster. It was applied to recreate the appearance of human skin and make the skulls look alive.

Instead of eyes the skulls had white shells placed in the sockets. There was even evidence that they had been painted. Why would people decorate skulls? Well, even though we live over 9,500 years later than these people, it's not hard to understand their reasons. When someone we love dies, it can be an incredibly sad time. In order to process this loss, we have to mourn. The beautiful thing about humans is that there is no single way to express our feelings. Some cultures bury their dead, some cremate those they've lost, some preserve their dead as mummies. In Neolithic Jericho they created **plaster skulls** of their loved ones.

Each plastered skull would have been known to the people that preserved it. They were real people who were sometimes happy and sometimes sad. Their lives were just as complicated as yours is today. Perhaps the seven skulls found by Kathleen's team made a family tree?

Thanks to Kathleen, we know so much more about people who lived in the Neolithic period. She also transformed archaeology in a more fundamental way. Together with Mortimer Wheeler, Kathleen developed a **new system of excavation** we still use today.

Archaeology is all about context. An artefact on its own tells us little, but if we know exactly where it came from and what it was found with, we can learn so much more! Kathleen and Mortimer decided to excavate in a grid system. The walls of the grid would be kept intact and never excavated. That way you could use them as a map to understand and date everything that you discovered. This simple but ingenious idea has provided us with so much knowledge about the ancient world!

THE PILLARS
OF GÖBEKLI TEPE

In 1994, German archaeologist Klaus Schmidt was looking for prehistoric sites in Turkey. He was reading through old excavation notes from the 1960s when he stumbled across a small mention of some **tombstones** from the medieval period (500 CE to 1500 CE). He decided to see them for himself.

As he unearthed the dirt around the tombstones he realised the notes had been seriously wrong... In front of him wasn't the ruins of something from the medieval period, but a 11,000-year-old prehistoric site! Klaus Schmidt was amazed at what he uncovered: huge **T-shaped pillars** decorated with arms, animals, and strange symbols. Göbekli Tepe, which means "Belly Hill" in Turkish, sits at the top of a large hill overlooking the vast plains below. Teams of German and Turkish archaeologists worked hard to unearth as much of the site as possible.

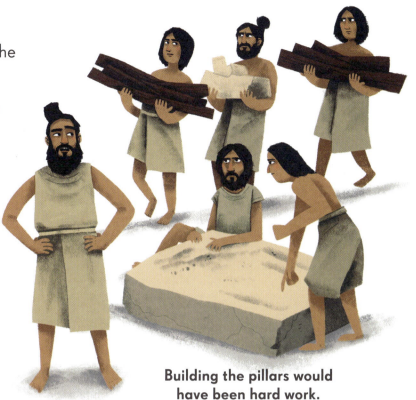

Building the pillars would have been hard work.

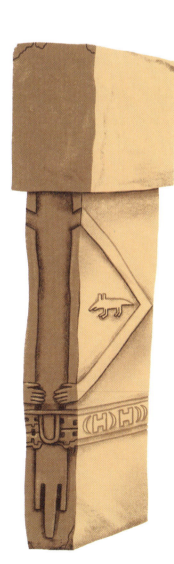

Each year of excavations revealed more giant T-shaped statues, all arranged in circles. Archaeologists believe these statues represent people. Can you see their arms and the belts around their waists? Many of the statues also have small animals on them. Archaeologists think they could signify **different tribes** or groups of people. What animal would you pick to represent your family? A lion or a bear? A slug?

Göbekli Tepe is about the same size as 13 football pitches. It's so big that it hasn't all been excavated – that will take another 50 years! Why did these people gather here to build it? Well, judging from the plants and animals found at the site, groups of people that were usually spread out across the landscape probably ventured to Göbekli Tepe at specific times of year to feast, drink, exchange information, and maybe even to find someone to fall in love with. With so much still to unearth, we will definitely be discovering incredible secrets from Göbekli Tepe for a long time to come.

THE MYSTERY OF THE STONES

In South West England sits one of most famous Neolithic monuments in the whole world – **Stonehenge**. At the height of its use, a whopping 4,500 years ago, 30 bus-sized stone structures called trilithons formed a circle inside an earthen bank. A trilithon is formed of two upright stones with another, a capstone, placed across the top. Inside this ring of trilithons, bluestones, each bigger than a person, formed a U-shape.

The capstones at Stonehenge are carved with joints to stop them falling over.

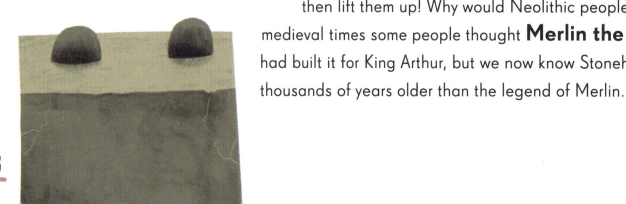

This incredible monument still stands today. Imagine how much effort it must have been to quarry the stones, shape them, carve joints in them to keep them in place, and then lift them up! Why would Neolithic people do this? In medieval times some people thought **Merlin the wizard** had built it for King Arthur, but we now know Stonehenge is thousands of years older than the legend of Merlin.

Digging in the centre of Stonehenge archaeologists have found 64 pits containing the cremated remains of ancient people. As many as 150 people were buried here. Perhaps Neolithic people gathered here to burn the dead and say goodbye to their loved ones? Stonehenge could also be a **giant calendar!** At midsummer the Sun rises over the largest stone at the site, the heel stone. While at midwinter the Sun sets between two of the large trilithons. The people who built Stonehenge were farmers, and knowing when the seasons changed was very important. Maybe they gathered here at these important times of year to throw large parties? Archaeologists have found lots of butchered animals that were probably part of a prehistoric barbecue.

The only thing we know for certain is that these prehistoric people, even with simple tools, were brilliant engineers.

Assembling Stonehenge was impressive, but there was another mystery that needed to be solved. How on earth did prehistoric people move the gigantic stones to the sacred site?

The large trilithons weigh as much as 45 tonnes (50 tons). To put it in context, that's about **the weight of a blue whale!** It would have taken many people and a lot of careful thought and planning to carve and lift them. However, the trilithons were taken from a quarry next to Stonehenge, so they didn't have too far to travel.

The smaller bluestones in the middle of Stonehenge on the other hand didn't look like any stone in the area. So where did they come from?

In 1923, a British geologist (that's someone who studies the Earth and the rocks found in it) called Henry Herbert Thomas was trying to answer that very question.

He searched the region around Stonehenge but none of the rocks in the area had the **distinctive blue colour**. As he explored around Britain he finally found a match to the bluestones. The only problem was it was in the Preseli Mountains of western Wales – about 140 miles (225 km) from Stonehenge!

When Henry first suggested this idea he was laughed at, as people didn't believe Neolithic farmers could have moved the stones so far. But modern geology and archaeology have proved Henry correct! We still don't know whether they moved the stones over land using logs, or over the sea. Maybe that's a mystery you can solve. Which do you think is more likely?

THE AMESBURY ARCHER

The area around Stonehenge is full of interesting prehistoric sites, including ceremonial roads, feasting sites, and burials. In 2002, builders were working on a housing development when they uncovered a skeleton in a grassy mound. At first the archaeologists thought the man found might have died in the Roman period. But as the team uncovered more of the body they found flint arrowheads, distinctive beaker-like bowls, boar tusks, and most importantly metal objects such as copper knives and gold hair ties. This grave was 4,300 years old – it was from the **Bronze Age!**

Wrist guard

Who was this mystery man? The key to his identity lay in the goods buried with him. He must have been a good archer, as he was buried with 18 arrowheads and wrist guards to protect his arms from the bow string. Being an archer was probably not his job, though. Hidden next to the boar tusks the team found a cushion stone. This is a small stone used as an anvil by the first metal workers, who would bash their metal on it. In the early days of metal working, the people who could produce metallic goods were held in high regard. They might even have been thought of as magicians.

Arrowheads

Boar tusks

Bowl

Flints

Gold hair ties

The body hid one more secret though. Have you ever heard the phrase "you are what you eat"? Well, in the food and water we consume are millions of different minerals. Minerals enter water as it runs along rocks, so each river has a unique signature depending on the rocks in the area. Analysis of the minerals in the Amesbury Archer's teeth shows he came from what is now **the Alps** in central Europe. Who knows how he ended up by Stonehenge, but this archery-loving, metal-working magician was certainly loved by his friends and family, because they gave him a king's burial!

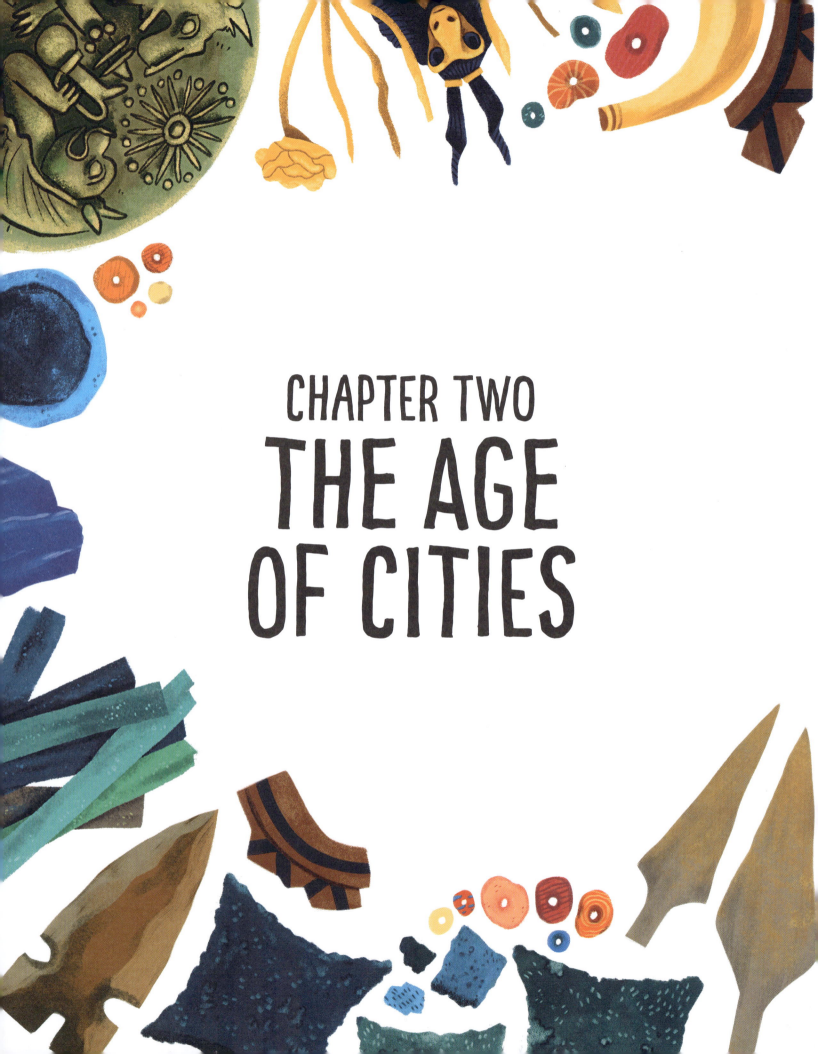

CHAPTER TWO
THE AGE OF CITIES

Five thousand years ago we enter an age of powerful kings and queens, legendary warriors, and rich merchants. By this point in history people in many parts of the world started living in cities for the first time, and craftspeople produced beautiful bronze artefacts – sometimes for trade, sometimes for war. Let's see what incredible treasures archaeologists have uncovered!

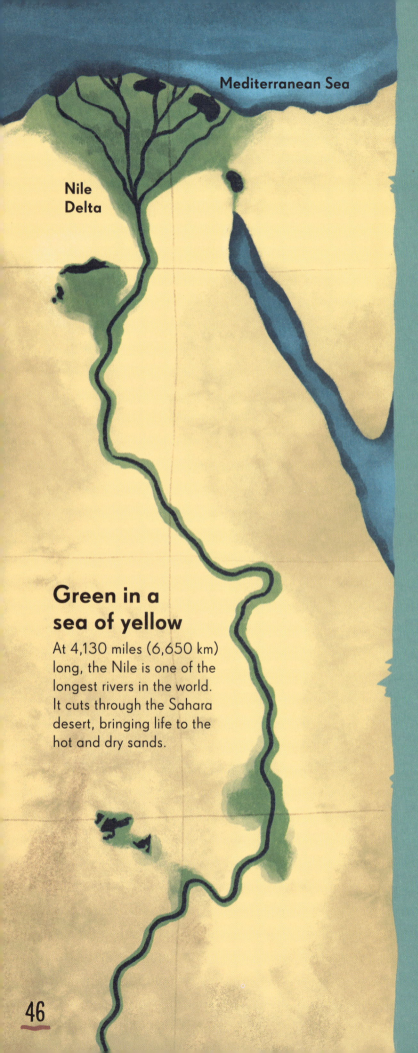

Mediterranean Sea

Nile Delta

TAKE A TRIP DOWN
THE NILE VALLEY

Let's take a cruise along the River Nile. Starting in the great lakes of West Africa you'll wind your way down towards the Mediterranean Sea. On the way you'll pass hungry hippos, angry crocodiles, and herds of elephants. You'll also journey through two of the most ancient kingdoms in the world: Egypt and Nubia.

Good farming

The Nile floods every year, depositing fresh soil and nutrients into the land around it. This allowed ancient Egypt and Nubia to grow wheat, flax, and papyrus. Trading wheat to its neighbours made ancient Egypt extremely wealthy.

Green in a sea of yellow

At 4,130 miles (6,650 km) long, the Nile is one of the longest rivers in the world. It cuts through the Sahara desert, bringing life to the hot and dry sands.

Wet highway

In the Bronze Age there weren't many roads, so lots of people travelled along rivers. Merchants transported food and animals, pharaohs built luxurious boats capable of carrying lots of servants, and craftspeople moved huge stones to build Egypt's great monuments.

Ancient Egyptians

The ancient Egyptians were one of the world's oldest civilisations, becoming a unified country in around 3100 BCE. They divided Egypt into two halves – Upper and Lower Egypt. The kingdom was ruled by a pharaoh, who the Egyptians believed was a god on Earth! The Egyptians had many gods who represented different aspects of life and nature.

The Egyptians had one of the earliest writing systems in the world, called hieroglyphs. Instead of letters they drew small pictures.

This means "Tutankhamun"

Anubis, the jackal, was god of the afterlife and lost souls.

Ramses II was one of the most famous Egyptian pharaohs. He was king for 66 years, built many huge monuments, and fought a lot of battles!

Mummies were stored in a stone coffin called a sarcophagus. Sometimes it was inscribed with curses to keep the dead safe from robbers.

When Egyptians died they performed a ritual called mummification. They removed the organs and wrapped up the body so it would last forever!

Early in Egyptian history the pharaohs built pyramids to protect their bodies for the afterlife. The biggest is the Great Pyramid of Giza.

THE TREASURES OF THE BOY PHARAOH

Three and a half thousand years ago the Valley of the Kings was the resting place of the Egyptian pharaohs. For 500 years the kings, queens, princes, and princesses of ancient Egypt were buried here in elaborate tombs. The walls of their graves were decorated with Egyptian gods and magical spells to guide them to the **afterlife**. Here, surrounded by their golden treasures, the royals lay for eternity.

At least that was the idea. Even though the Egyptians tried hard to hide their tombs and keep their dead kings safe, over time their tombs had been robbed for their gold. By the year 1922, many thought all the tombs had been discovered.

Underneath the hot desert sun Englishman **Howard Carter** had been digging in the valley for six years, hoping to find a tomb that hadn't been robbed. He had found nothing and time was running out. He only had the money to dig this one last year. One day, a young Egyptian boy was bringing water to the diggers when he tripped and fell over a stone. He probably thought he was in trouble for spilling everyone's drinks, but he was about to change history...

As they cleared the rubble around the rock, they discovered a staircase heading down into the ground. At the bottom of the stairs Howard was to make the discovery of his lifetime. The tomb of Tutankhamun!

As Howard and his team entered the tomb an incredible site awaited them. "Wonderful things!", Howard muttered as his light shone off the gold of Tutankhamun's treasures. The tomb was packed to the ceiling with everything a king would need for the afterlife. Jewellery, chairs, beds, a chariot, weapons, more than a hundred pairs of spare underpants – everything his heart could desire.

At the centre of it all was the mummy of King Tutankhamun himself! On his head was an **elaborate gold mask**. The Egyptians believed in preserving the body for the afterlife and they would spare no expense to stop it from rotting.

The process took 70 days. First they would remove all your organs. They would scoop your brain out of your nose using a little hook! All of these organs would be placed in little jars. Only your heart would be left in place – as ancient Egyptians believed this was the essential part of your being and must remain.

As Howard examined the body of the pharaoh he realised the king was very young. Tutankhamun was only nine years old when he became king, but died when he was 18. How the boy king died has puzzled archaeologists for a hundred years.

Some wondered if he fell off a chariot. Egyptian kings often rode chariots when they were hunting or fighting a battle. They were extremely fast and dangerous. X-rays revealed that King Tut had an injury to the back of the head. A new theory emerged – maybe he was murdered! As it turned out, this particular injury was probably the result of someone clumsy unwrapping his mummy.

TUTANKHAMUN MAY HAVE INJURED HIMSELF CHARIOT RACING

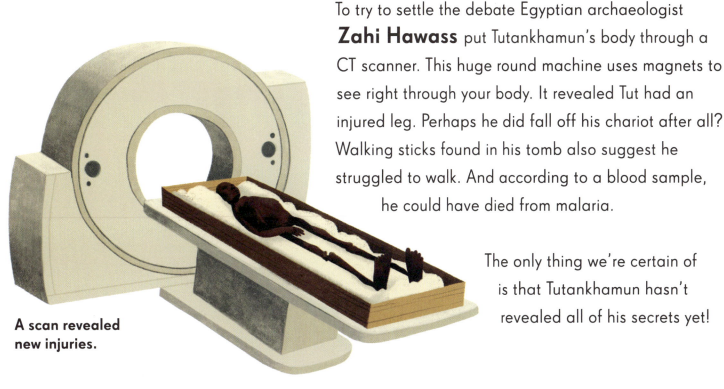

A scan revealed new injuries.

To try to settle the debate Egyptian archaeologist **Zahi Hawass** put Tutankhamun's body through a CT scanner. This huge round machine uses magnets to see right through your body. It revealed Tut had an injured leg. Perhaps he did fall off his chariot after all? Walking sticks found in his tomb also suggest he struggled to walk. And according to a blood sample, he could have died from malaria.

The only thing we're certain of is that Tutankhamun hasn't revealed all of his secrets yet!

THE KINGDOM OF KUSH

As you head south on the great river Nile, past the Egyptian pyramids, past the Valley of the Kings, and over five sets of wild rapids, you'll eventually reach the ancient Kingdom of Kush, a place with an unparalleled collection of famous buildings. The capital of Kush was the city of Meroë. From here great kings, called **Qore**, ruled the kingdom. They traded goods with Egypt, the Mediterranean, and the heart of Africa. As they were Egypt's neighbour for thousands of years, many of their beliefs were the same. They worshipped some of the same gods, such as Isis, the goddess of life and the Moon. Kush and Egypt were so close that they were sometimes ruled by the same pharaoh, like Taharqa, the statue on the right, who was Qore of Kush and pharaoh of Egypt from 690 BCE.

52

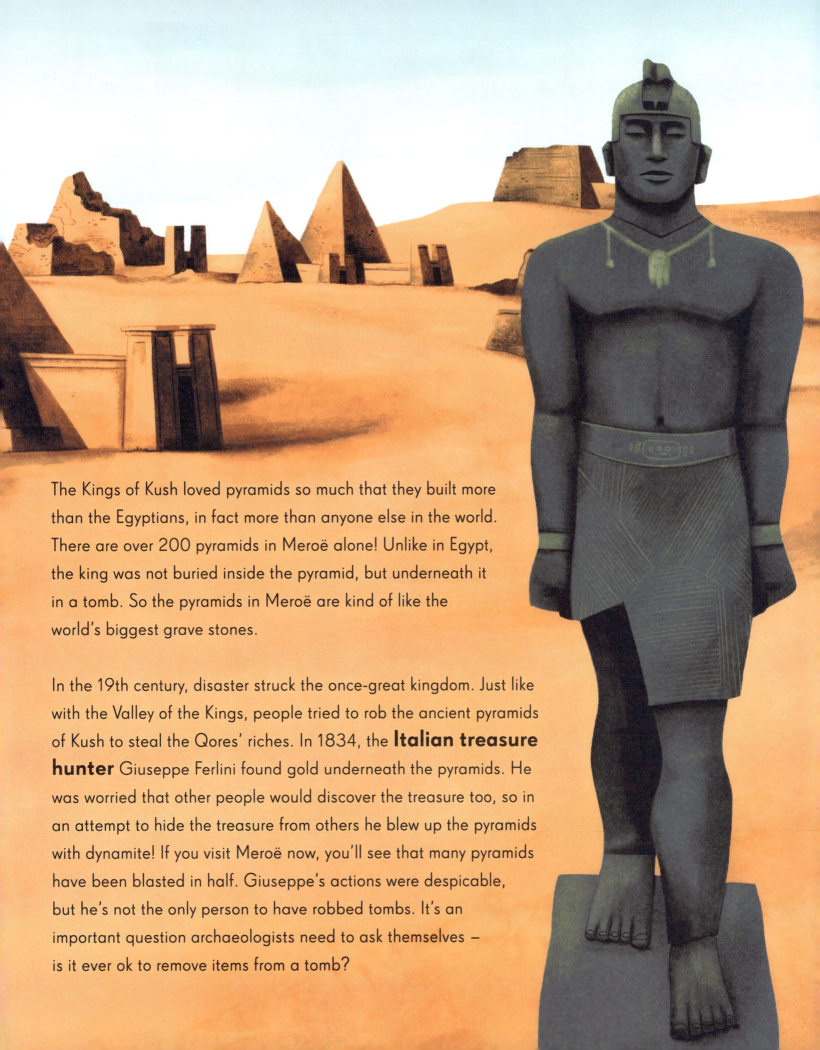

The Kings of Kush loved pyramids so much that they built more than the Egyptians, in fact more than anyone else in the world. There are over 200 pyramids in Meroë alone! Unlike in Egypt, the king was not buried inside the pyramid, but underneath it in a tomb. So the pyramids in Meroë are kind of like the world's biggest grave stones.

In the 19th century, disaster struck the once-great kingdom. Just like with the Valley of the Kings, people tried to rob the ancient pyramids of Kush to steal the Qores' riches. In 1834, the **Italian treasure hunter** Giuseppe Ferlini found gold underneath the pyramids. He was worried that other people would discover the treasure too, so in an attempt to hide the treasure from others he blew up the pyramids with dynamite! If you visit Meroë now, you'll see that many pyramids have been blasted in half. Giuseppe's actions were despicable, but he's not the only person to have robbed tombs. It's an important question archaeologists need to ask themselves — is it ever ok to remove items from a tomb?

THE SLEEPING ARMY

The year was 1974, and it was a hot and dry summer in China – the country was experiencing a terrible drought. Archaeologist Zhao Kangmin was sat in his office when the phone rang. Farmers had been digging a deep well to try and get some desperately needed water when they unearthed some **terracotta heads**. Zhao was intrigued.

These farmers lived in Xi'an, in the shadow of one of China's most important ancient monuments, the tomb of the first emperor, Qin. Zhao Kangmin had dug in the region before and found two statues of kneeling crossbowmen. He headed out to see what the farmers had discovered, but even with his knowledge of the area he would be astounded at what they had uncovered – the Terracotta Army!

Archaeologists examined the heads and decided to expand the excavation. As their shovels cleared the dry earth they found more. Not just one or two soldiers but hundreds! As it stands today archaeologists have unearthed over 1,900 terracotta soldiers and they're still going. There may be as many as 7,000 terracotta soldiers buried in Xi'an.

Archaeologists digging around the soldiers have found terracotta representations of all aspects of life during Emperor Qin's reign. Government officials to administer his empire, musicians to play his favourite songs, and dancing acrobats to entertain the emperor when he was bored. Clearly Emperor Qin was determined that his life on Earth was carried forward into the **afterlife**. According to legend, he was so concerned about death that he sent thousands of youngsters on a mission to find herbs of immortality that lay on three islands to the east of China. Unfortunately for the emperor there are no herbs of immortality, and in the year 210 BCE he was laid to rest with his terracotta world.

THE RANKS OF THE
TERRACOTTA ARMY

The Terracotta Army was a fitting bodyguard for China's first emperor. Over 7,000 soldiers stand guard outside his tomb, still ready for battle even after over 2,000 years under the ground. They're a brilliant example of the ingenuity of ancient Chinese craftspeople. Although all the soldiers appear unique, they were actually mass-produced. By making the soldiers in different pieces, the craftsmen could mix and match parts, giving the impression that each soldier was crafted individually. Each part was stamped with the name of the person who made it, to help track any mistakes.

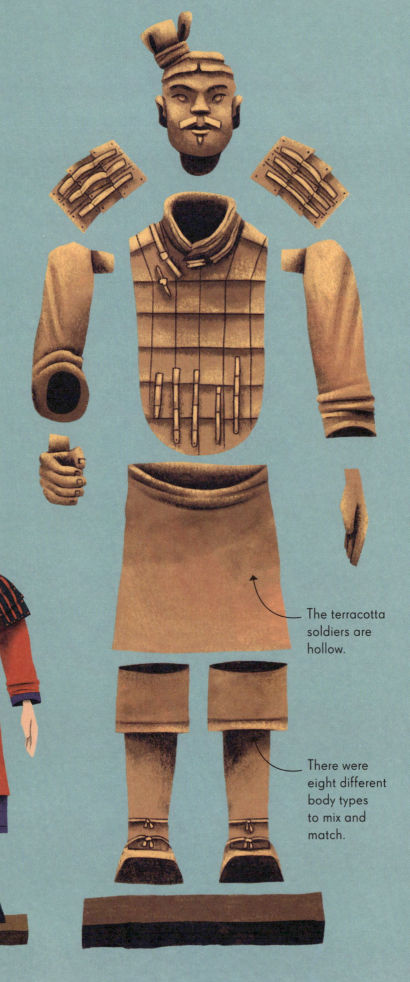

The soldiers wore armour made up of riveted pieces of metal and leather.

The terracotta soldiers are hollow.

There were eight different body types to mix and match.

Paint job

Although they all appear to be the brown colour of terracotta now, if you look closely you can still see traces of paint on the soldiers. When they were finished, seeing the 7,000 soldiers lined up in their bright red uniforms must have been an incredible sight.

Archers

Archers are positioned throughout the army. They would have once carried impressive crossbows, but these have rotted away. The archers wear their hair in a topknot.

Standing archer

Kneeling archer

Cavalry

So far over 600 cavalry soldiers have been unearthed, each one standing next to a life-size terracotta horse!

Charioteers

A hundred chariots were buried with Emperor Qin. The chariots carried officers around the battlefield, allowing them to race around and shout commands at their troops.

General

Officers that were buried in the tomb were made slightly taller than regular soldiers, with generals being the tallest of them all. (Though surely there were some short generals in real life!)

THE SECRETS OF EMPEROR QIN'S TOMB

The full name of China's first emperor was **Qin Shi Huangdi**, which translates as "the first emperor of Qin (China)". Qin transformed Chinese society. Before him, China was made up of several warring kingdoms, but Qin wanted to rule over the entire land. To achieve this, Qin and his chief minister, Li Si, revolutionised their small kingdom. All soldiers were given the same weapons to cut costs. He standardised the Chinese alphabet so his people, no matter where they were from, could communicate. And he built canals and granaries to move and feed his growing army.

As a result of these changes Qin unified all of China. He did not rest though, but turned his attention to building the largest tomb in the entire world. As well as the Terracotta Army he also built the **world's largest pyramid** to contain his tomb. According to records he mobilized over 700,000 people to build it! Qin was not a man who was happy with the simple things in life.

It's easy for stories of great kings and queens to become exaggerated over time, their achievements becoming legend. Apparently, underneath Qin's pyramid, workers built a replica model of China. Qin's body was placed in the centre of a map and rivers of **mercury** (a special liquid metal the Chinese considered the elixir of life) flowed into a recreated sea.

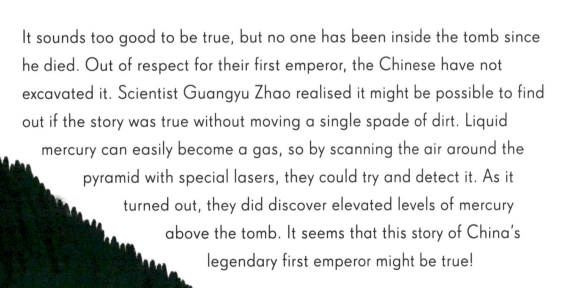

It sounds too good to be true, but no one has been inside the tomb since he died. Out of respect for their first emperor, the Chinese have not excavated it. Scientist Guangyu Zhao realised it might be possible to find out if the story was true without moving a single spade of dirt. Liquid mercury can easily become a gas, so by scanning the air around the pyramid with special lasers, they could try and detect it. As it turned out, they did discover elevated levels of mercury above the tomb. It seems that this story of China's legendary first emperor might be true!

THE WONDERS OF THE
INDUS VALLEY

Modern India and Pakistan are incredible lands, full of diverse cultures, languages, and religions. The earliest of all civilisations in this region was the Indus Valley Civilisation. Reaching its height around 2600 BCE, it was one of the largest Bronze Age cultures in the entire world – bigger than ancient Egypt and Mesopotamia combined!

Nice pad

If you were to go back in time, you might want to pick the Indus Valley. Everyone had nice houses – even those who didn't have high status in society. You would have had toilets, water, and a bathroom for showers. For normal people to have access to such comforts was really unique for the time.

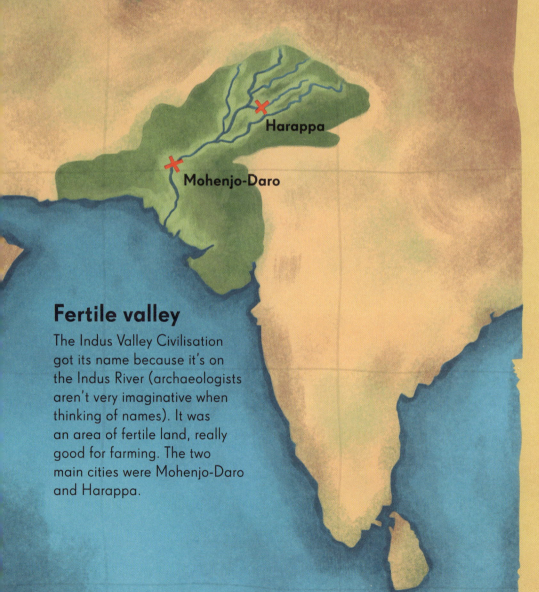

Harappa

Mohenjo-Daro

Fertile valley

The Indus Valley Civilisation got its name because it's on the Indus River (archaeologists aren't very imaginative when thinking of names). It was an area of fertile land, really good for farming. The two main cities were Mohenjo-Daro and Harappa.

Trading gems

Trade was the life blood of the cities on the Indus. They even built colonies in far away lands to extract precious resources, such as lapis lazuli. They didn't use this blue stone themselves, but mined it to trade with people who did.

The Great Bath

In the city of Mohenjo-Daro the inhabitants built a huge bath. It was lined with square nooks. Were they changing rooms? Rooms to relax? Or were they little chapels to worship their gods? It's hard to say for sure.

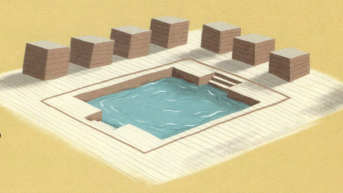

Life on the river

Travelling on the rivers of India and Pakistan would have been an almost daily occurance in the Indus Valley. Trade, communication, transport – everything revolved around the river.

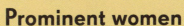

Prominent women

The ancient people of the Indus Valley created many statues of women. Some are richly dressed with jewellery, others are clearly playing or dancing. We're not sure exactly what they mean, but it's clear women had a significant public role in society.

Warriors?

Archaeologists have long debated how peaceful life was on the Indus. Were the people there wild warriors or peaceful merchants? Many houses contained spears and axes, which probably weren't used to bake cakes.

THE RIDDLES OF MOHENJO-DARO

In 1919, R.D. Banerji was working for the Archaeological Survey of India. His mission was to find and identify unknown ancient sites. As he explored an area of what is now central Pakistan he found a **Buddhist stupa**, dating to the year 300 CE. A stupa is a round building where Buddhists store the precious relics of their most important monks and teachers.

Banerji was an energetic and accomplished archaeologist. As he pottered around the site, more and more things started to stand out to him. The stupa seemed to have been built on a mound made up of two distinct layers. One was built by the Buddhists, but who built the bottom layer? He wandered around the site more (the first step in an archaeological investigation is to walk across the site, just to see what is lying on the surface). As he walked he noticed a flint scraper. But flint tools were not used in 300 CE... He realised he was dealing with a much more ancient site and decided to excavate.

As Banerji dug down he found two ancient tablets with **mysterious writing** on them. It was then he truly realised what he had discovered - an ancient city from the Indus Valley Civilisation! Over the next 20 years Indian and British archaeologists excavated the whole site. As it would turn out this would be the largest ancient city ever discovered in India, Mohenjo-Daro.

Mohenjo-Daro was a huge place. At its height there were probably 50,000 people living in the city. It was constructed on two large mounds. On top of one mound were public buildings, a bath, a possible granary, and maybe a college. The second was more residential. Hundreds of houses lined streets **orientated to the points of a compass**. This was a huge project – whoever was in charge was an accomplished engineer.

As for the two tablets Banerji found, the tablets with the mysterious writing? Well, they're still a mystery. To this day we have no idea what they say. Imagine if someone handed you a text written in a foreign language. Could you work out what it means without a dictionary? It would be extremely hard! Experts can't even agree how many letters were in the Indus Valley alphabet. Estimates vary wildly – some say around 149, others 537! The big difficulty is that we can't be sure if we're looking at different letters, or if people just had **different handwriting**. Most of the letters are all carved onto clay seals. This has given archaeologists and linguists a small clue as to what they mean.

Some could have been used to give out different goods, almost like money. Perhaps you could go to the granary with your inscription and they would give you bread. Other seals had hoops on the back, which suggests they might have been worn like a badge of office. In the same way we have police badges and ID cards, perhaps Indus people had seals describing their jobs, like "Farmer", "Scribe", or "Merchant".

Carving the tablets

The seals have many images of animals on them. Elephants, rhinos, tigers, and most commonly a bull... or maybe it's a unicorn. Take a look at the seals on the left. One clearly shows an elephant, another a bull, but two show an animal with just one horn. Are we looking at a bull from the side, or is it a unicorn? Archaeologists can't agree and the **bull versus unicorn debate** has been raging for over 100 years! What do you think it is?

You can have a go at deciphering the riddles of Indus Valley language yourself. Below is an **ancient Indus seal** with seven different symbols on it. Two stick people, two slightly different crosses, a jar, a fish, and another jar. Archaeologists have worked out that the script is read from right to left, so start there and have a guess. Linguists (language experts) working on this exact inscription have different theories. One thinks it says, "Here is the tribute offered to the god Kueya", while another has suggested, "The aquatic birds have covered all the waterways". Other suggestions include "The mountain worshipped one" and "Three Great Buffalo".

As you can see there is little agreement amongst experts. Which of the translations looks best to you?

WARFARE IN THE
BRONZE AGE

As you've seen, the Bronze Age was a time of fantastic art and powerful rulers. It wasn't always so peaceful though. If there's one thing powerful kings and queens love to do, it's fight. Warfare was common as rulers fought with each other for control of cities and trade routes – and the wealth that came with them. In the archaeological record we have found tonnes of evidence of conflict. Let's take a look at some great examples from the eastern Mediterranean.

City walls

If your neighbours are trying to steal your stuff, the first thing to do is build something to stop them. As warfare increased, many cities built huge walls to protect themselves.

Hittite chariots

The Hittite empire was one of ancient Egypt's fiercest rivals, and its deadliest weapon was the war chariot. Each chariot could hold three people: a driver, a soldier armed with a spear or bow, and a shield bearer. The Hittite king could send thousands of chariots into battle!

Trojan Horse

Many battles have become shrouded in myth – a perfect example is the story of the Trojan Horse. It is said Greek soldiers hid inside a giant wooden horse, allowing them to sneak into the city of Troy and take it from the Trojans. We're not sure if this really happened, but dreadful sieges were common in the Bronze Age.

Spectacular armour

The best example of armour from the Bronze Age is the Dendra Panoply. It's a full suit of bronze armour, topped with a helmet made of boar's teeth! The Greek warrior who owned it must have been incredibly strong to wear so much armour.

Egyptian archers

Archers were a common feature of war. Hundreds, if not thousands, of soldiers would launch arrow after arrow at the enemy. The Egyptian army had a force of archers called the Pitati. Many of these archers came from Kush and Nubia to the south of Egypt.

THE TOMB OF THE GRIFFIN WARRIOR

The archaeologists were waiting under a tarpaulin for the rain to stop. The digging season had not been going well so far. They were excavating in the shadow of the ancient **Palace of Nestor**, a Bronze Age building on Greece's southwest coast. The team had hoped to explore a promising site but were unable to get the correct permits, so they settled on an unassuming olive grove further along the hill.

When the rain stopped they returned to work. Despite the downpour the ground was still rock hard and the archaeologists had to smash through the clay with pickaxes. They were excavating a cluster of rocks about the size of a grave. As they dug deeper and deeper, the outline of a tomb became clear. Flint Dibble, the archaeologist wielding the pickaxe, moved a stone, and underneath it was something far more precious than mud. He had found a piece of bronze. Flint called over his colleague Alison Fields. They knew they had stumbled upon something special, but at this point they didn't yet realise they were standing on the tomb of a warrior from the **Mycenaean period** of Greek history, which stretched from around 1600 BCE to 1100 BCE.

This warrior had died 3,500 years ago. His friends and family decided to bury him with extremely lavish riches: gold

rings, a bronze sword and dagger, a helmet made of boar tusks, and a disc engraved with two griffins. The archaeologists named the man the "Griffin Warrior".

The objects in this tomb are not just beautiful, they also tell us a lot about the past. For 100 years, archaeologists have debated whether Mycenaean Greece and the **Minoan civilisation** on the nearby island of Crete were in contact with each other. The objects buried with the Griffin Warrior were found in a Mycenaean tomb, but are typical of Minoan art. This shows that rich and powerful Mycenaeans were definitely interacting with the Minoans.

Why bury so much wealth in a tomb? Well according to Flint Dibble, it's all about the experience. Burying someone and throwing such a lavish funeral is a powerful experience for those taking part. It helps build and establish social ties, bringing people together. It's also an experience for the archaeologists digging it up 3,500 years later. One that Flint and Alison will surely never forget!

The disc the Griffin Warrior was named after

THE FIRST CITIES OF
MESOPOTAMIA

In the Bronze Age the first true cities emerged in the Middle East, in a region called Mesopotamia. Ur, Nineveh, Babylon, Uruk, and Aššur were centres of trade and empires, vibrant cities full of people, exotic goods, and fearsome rulers. These cities had lots in common, but that doesn't mean they were friendly. They frequently fought wars and competed against each other. Each city had its own rulers and different gods. Let's take a look at Ur, founded in 3800 BCE. It might just be the oldest city in the world!

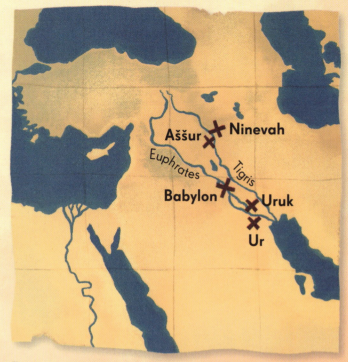

Between two rivers

Mesopotamia is Greek for "land between rivers". The Tigris and Euphrates rivers flow through the region on their way to the Persian Gulf, a sea to the south, providing the perfect conditions for farming and trade.

The Ziggurat of Ur

At the centre of Ur was a huge ziggurat. Ziggurats were enormous temples made up of different levels. As you went up, each level was a little smaller than the last, making the ziggurat slightly resemble a pyramid. At Ur the outside bricks may have been glazed and brightly coloured. At the top was a shrine where the priests of the city performed the most important rituals.

Early writing

The people of Mesopotamia wrote in a language we call cuneiform. They would use a small stick to draw symbols in clay. The tablet was then dried or baked and the message preserved (luckily for us). Cuneiform eventually evolved into an alphabet of letters made up of small triangles.

The Standard of Ur

The Standard of Ur is one of the greatest treasures ever uncovered by archaeologists. Incredibly it's a mosaic about 4,600 years old, and shows different scenes from the royal palace at Ur. It has two sides: peace and war. On the peace side you can see farmers and traders bringing fish and animals to the king. On the war side, soldiers hold their swords in preparation for battle.

THE BURIAL OF QUEEN PUABI

In 1922 British archaeologists Leonard and Katherine Woolley and their team of Iraqi excavators started digging in the ancient Mesopotamian city of **Ur**. Little did they realise how much sand they would have to remove. Shovel after shovel, bucket after bucket, deeper and deeper they went. As deep as three or four houses – so deep they had to build stairs just to get out!

Eventually they hit something. There, buried for thousands of years under the hot desert sand, was the tomb of Queen Puabi, a super-rich ruler who lived around 4,600 years ago.

Queen Puabi's tomb was full of incredible treasures, including golden cups for drinking beer (which Mesopotamians adored and wrote songs about) and wooden lyres, a type of ancient instrument. The people of Ur loved music and poetry. Some of their poems, such as the epic of **Gilgamesh**, are still known today.

Ram statuette

Golden cup

Lyre

After over 4,000 years underneath all that sand Queen Puabi and her servants were as flat as a pancake. Fortunately, after many hours of careful work, Katherine Woolley was able to reconstruct them. This gives us a brilliant idea of how rich Mesopotamian women would have dressed thousands of years ago. Lots of elaborate gold headbands, earrings, and incredible necklaces – and big hair!

"Servants?" I hear you ask. That's right. As Leonard and his team were digging around the tomb they uncovered a grisly sight. Queen Puabi was buried with **52 servants.** Guards, horsemen, female attendants – everyone the queen needed to help her in the afterlife.

How did all these people die, everyone wondered? Next to each body excavators found a small cup. Katherine mused whether they'd all been poisoned after following the queen into the tomb. Recent examinations of the skulls of the servants have shown they had also been hit on their heads. Who knows, maybe it was both? And all in service of their queen.

Queen Puabi and a servant

THE OLDEST LETTER OF COMPLAINT

Have you ever bought anything you weren't happy with? Cold French fries at a fast-food restaurant, a new computer game that doesn't work properly, or a pencil that just keeps breaking no matter how many times you sharpen it? It's frustrating isn't it? I'm sure you've complained, or at least thought about it. Well, dear reader, you are in good company. Humans have been complaining about **poor customer service** since the early days of writing!

Leonard Woolley (yes, the same chap who discovered Queen Puabi) was digging at a different location in the city of Ur. As he removed piles of sand he discovered a seriously ancient house. It was almost 4,000 years old.

Hidden in the corner of this building was a **very peculiar letter**. It wasn't from a king or queen, and it didn't tell of heroic deeds and glorious battles – it was a letter of complaint written by a man called Nanni to a copper dealer called Ea-nasir! Here's an excerpt:

When you came, you said to me as follows: "I will give Gimil-Sin (when he comes) fine quality copper ingots". You left then but you did not do what you promised me. You put ingots that were not good before my messenger (Sit-Sin) and said: "If you want to take them, take them; if you do not want to take them, go away!" What do you take me for, that you treat somebody like me with such contempt...

Basically what it's saying is: the copper you sold me is rubbish, you treated my servant like an idiot, and if you want to sell me copper again, you'll have to come to my house!

TRADE IN THE MEDITERRANEAN

Today, we tend to think of seas as things that get in the way. In the Bronze Age, however, travelling over land was incredibly hard. There were very few roads, and horses and carts were slow. There were also no police or mobile phones – you could very easily be robbed as soon as you left your village! As a result most trade was done over water, especially around the Mediterranean Sea.

Copper ingots

Copper and tin were metals essential for the production of bronze. But annoyingly they were never found in the same place! Spain, which had natural copper, traded it in blocks called ingots.

Sea snails

Three thousand years ago, if your clothes were covered in crushed snails, you were extremely fashionable. One sea snail in particular created a very bright purple colour when it was crushed. Merchants in North Africa grew rich trading this purple dye to Bronze Age royalty.

Amber

People loved making jewellery out of amber, but it only comes from northern Europe. Merchants would travel south to Italy and exchange it for goods they couldn't get in the north, like wine.

Greek pottery

All around the Mediterranean you can find ancient Greek pottery. Merchants would fill pots with olive oil, wine, and fish to be enjoyed at fancy banquets.

Lebanese cedar

All of this trade wouldn't be possible without ships made from Lebanese cedar. It was the best wood for making boats and was very expensive.

Glass rods

Ancient Egyptians were particularly skilled at making glass, but not everyone wanted to wear Egyptian-style jewellery. Craftspeople would buy rods of coloured Egyptian glass and turn them into something more to their taste.

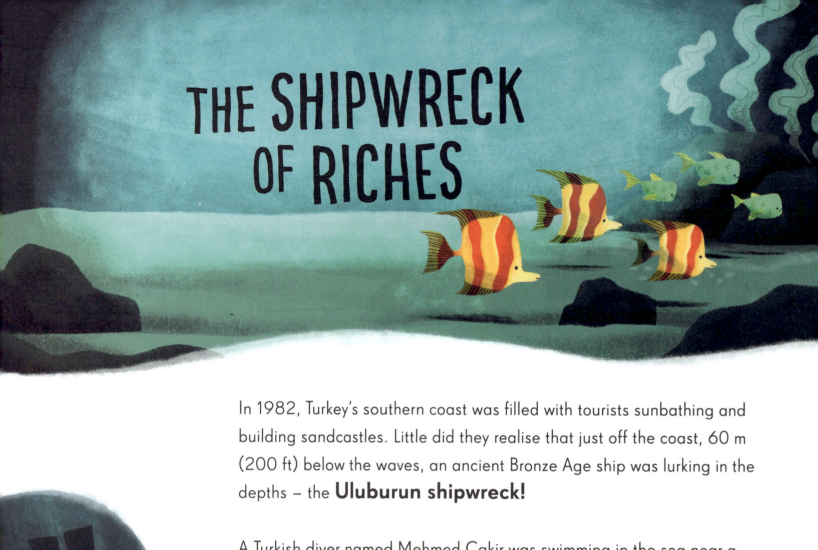

THE SHIPWRECK OF RICHES

In 1982, Turkey's southern coast was filled with tourists sunbathing and building sandcastles. Little did they realise that just off the coast, 60 m (200 ft) below the waves, an ancient Bronze Age ship was lurking in the depths – the **Uluburun shipwreck!**

A Turkish diver named Mehmed Çakir was swimming in the sea near a small town called Bodrum. He was looking for sea sponges (they're a bit like coral). Instead of finding a nice natural way to clean, he found what he described as "metal biscuits with ears". These weren't biscuits though, but ancient blocks of tin called ingots. The local archaeologists were notified and an expedition to recover the wreck began.

As the wreck was so deep below the waves, nobody had seen it since 1300 BCE – that's over 3,000 years ago! Fortunately this meant the contents of the ship were in incredible condition. The team found 175 pieces of glass in four different colours: blue, turquoise, purple, and yellow. There were 70,000 beads, destined to be turned into fine jewellery,

not to mention 24 elephant tusks and 14 hippopotamus teeth! Still preserved were razor-sharp bronze swords from Italy, spices, herbs, snail shells for dyes, gold, amber... everything a Bronze Age trading vessel could carry.

Such an incredible haul presented serious challenges to the archaeologists. The wreck was so deep they could only dive for short periods of time, meaning they couldn't excavate much in one go.

In the end the divers had to dive 22,400 times to recover everything! It took them **11 years** to recover the treasure. Can you imagine working on one thing for so long?

Once the treasure was recovered, the real investigation began. Who were the sailors on the ship? Where were they going? And what were they doing with all that treasure?

Jars

Copper ingots

Glass and beads

No bodies were found in the wreck. Maybe the sailors survived and swam to shore, or maybe they became **fish food?** We can get an idea of the identity of the people from what they left behind. Archaeologists found four sets of weights similar to those found in modern Israel and Lebanon. These were used to measure quantities of goods, just like the scales at a grocer's. In ancient times the people from this region were called Canaanites and Phoenicians. We don't know if all the crew came from that region, but it seems as though at least four of them did.

Where were they going? Well, considering the position of the ship it seems it was travelling west, in the direction of two great civilisations of the Bronze Age: the **Minoans** of Crete and the **Mycenaeans** of mainland Greece. The ship may have been heading to their famous royal palaces. Rulers in the Bronze Age sent each other elaborate gifts to keep the peace, help to negotiate treaties, or even to make alliances against their enemies. The goods in the ship closely match the items mentioned in letters by Pharaoh Akhenaten, who was King of Egypt at the time. (Fun fact, he was Tutankhamun's father!) Was he sending gifts to a Minoan king?

As to why the ship sank – at the minute we don't know. Sailing in the Bronze Age was very dangerous. A storm could easily damage the ships. Perhaps the sailors were caught one night by a **tsunami**, throwing them into the cold, dark water. That's a mystery for future archaeologists to solve!

CHAPTER THREE
ANCIENT EMPIRES

We've now come forward in time to around 2,000 years ago. In Europe and Africa the Roman Empire spread its tentacles across the land. In Asia, nomadic horsemen were on the march from the borders of China to the Caucasus Mountains. In the Americas, they were building: from the huge pyramids of the Maya, to the largest snake in the entire world. Adventure awaits!

THE KINGDOMS OF
THE MAYA

In the heart of Central America was one of the most fascinating civilisations to have ever existed. A land of tall pyramids, powerful rulers, and ancient astronomers. The world of the Maya! Let's take a look at the archaeology of these ancient cities as we explore what made the Maya civilisation so unique.

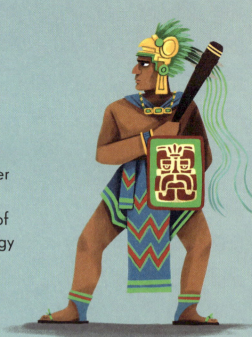

Rulers

Each Maya city had a ruler who lived in a palace in the centre of town. They had to participate in sacred rituals on behalf of their people, some of which included the spilling of human blood.

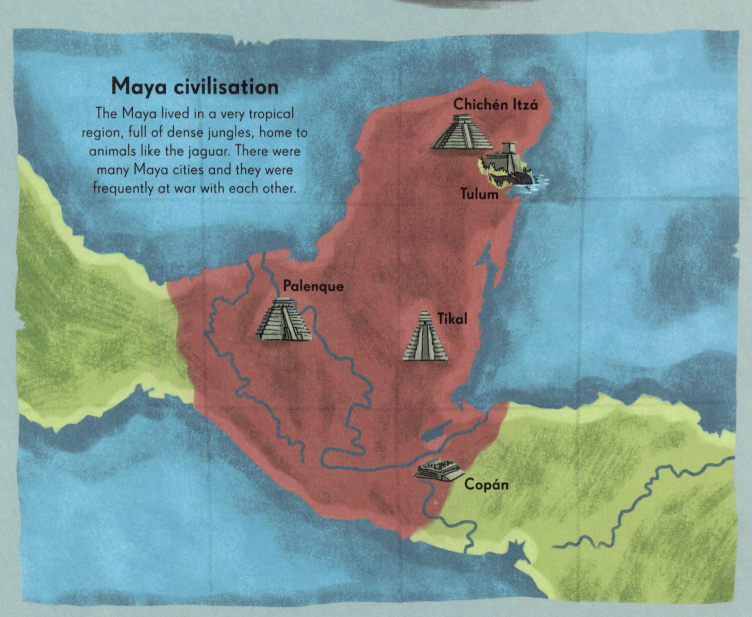

Maya civilisation

The Maya lived in a very tropical region, full of dense jungles, home to animals like the jaguar. There were many Maya cities and they were frequently at war with each other.

Chichén Itzá

Tulum

Palenque

Tikal

Copán

Calendar

The Maya had a sophisticated calendar that consisted of different cycles. They had a 365-day cycle called the *Haab*, which is roughly the same as our year, but was divided into 19 months.

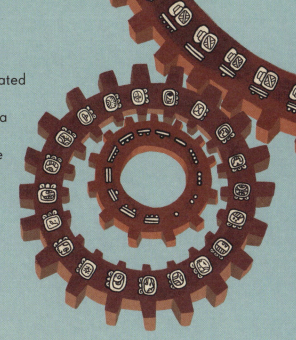

Writing system

The Maya developed a writing system made of different pictures called glyphs. Through these we can learn loads about Maya society. The glyphs on the top row mean "white" and "sky" (from left to right). The bottom symbols mean "jaguar" and "yellow".

Women

Women had an important role in Maya society, producing textiles and food, and participating in religious ceremonies. Unfortunately they are rarely mentioned in texts, but we know some women would become queens of Maya cities, such as Lady Wac Chanil Ahau of Naranjo.

Corn god

Hun Hunahpu was the Maya god of maize (aka corn). According to Maya religion, his blood and corn were what made human life possible. He wasn't the only god though. The Maya worshipped many deities, such as Chac the rain god and Kisin – "the flatulant one" – the god of death and decay.

Chichén Itzá

Chichén Itzá was one of the largest cities in the Maya world. At its centre sits the "Temple of Kukulcán", a huge pyramid. At the top is the Throne of the Red Jaguar – probably the seat of Chichén Itzá's rulers.

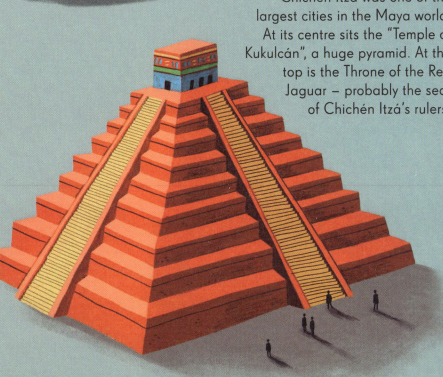

THE SECRET AT THE TEMPLE OF INSCRIPTIONS

Deep in the sweltering jungle of south Mexico there was once a great bustling city called Palenque. It was one of the most important cities in all of ancient Maya civilisation. In 615 CE, Palenque was about to get a new ruler. But there was something a bit different about this king – he was only 12 years old! **K'inich Janaab Pakal**, or Pakal for short, was so young that at the start his mum, Queen Sak K'uk', helped him rule the city. It just goes to show, even kings have to listen to their mums sometimes...

The Maya loved art, science, and sports. From Pakal's palace he could watch two teams play a popular game with a rubber ball in a giant stone court. A bit like a mix between football and basketball, it was not for the faint-hearted – **sometimes the losers were executed**. Players were highly skilled, using their hips to manoeuvre the ball through stone hoops high up on the sides of the court.

When Pakal became king the city of Palenque was in trouble. They had just lost a war and Pakal's father had died. Pakal proved a wise ruler, though. He built a brand-new palace and several impressive temples. Not only that, but he knew how to win a battle. In the year 659 CE, Pakal defeated the rulers of six other cities and Palenque became the **most powerful kingdom** in the region.

For years archaeologists battled mosquitoes and thick vines to explore
the ruins of Palenque to try to discover more about Pakal's reign. In 1949,
Mexican archaeologist **Alberto Ruz Lhuiller** was working on one of
Pakal's greatest buildings, the Temple of Inscriptions. It got that name from
all the writing on the walls. Alberto noticed a giant stone on the floor that
had 12 small holes. *How strange*, he thought. He got to work lifting the
stone and discovered a secret staircase! That was the good news. The bad
news was someone had filled the staircase with lots of stones and mud. It
took four years to reach the bottom, but it was worth the wait. After years of
digging, Alberto made a fantastic discovery. The tomb of King Pakal himself!

King Pakal was buried in a massive stone sarcophagus (that's a big fancy box for dead people). On the front was a picture of Pakal, dressed as the god of corn. Corn was the most important food for the Maya and they ate it every day. Inside the sarcophagus was the king, wearing a beautiful mask made from a green stone called **jade**. Rich Maya loved this stone and Pakal was no different.

Alberto realised it was possible to take the lid off Pakal's sarcophagus, meaning the dead king's body was probably brought out for special occasions. You may think that taking a dead

body to a party sounds surprising, but to the Maya, the king had a special connection to their gods and ancestors. Even after the king was dead, he was still loved and respected. From reading the writing on the wall and the tomb, Alberto discovered that Pakal had built the temple when he was 70 years old. He had lived to the ripe old age of 81, and had been king for a staggering 63 years! No longer a child king, he had become the legend **Pakal the Great**.

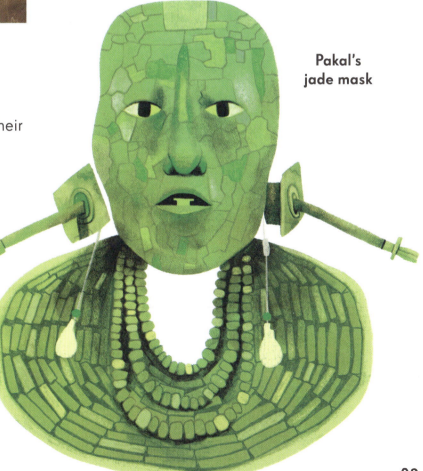

Pakal's jade mask

THE DANGERS OF
RISING WATER

Nearly three quarters of Earth's surface is covered in water. We drink it, wash with it, and live next to it. But water can be peaceful one minute and destructive the next. Tsunamis, rising sea levels, and rogue waves are testament to nature's awesome power.

Port Royal

In the 17th century, Port Royal in Jamaica was a pirate's paradise. But on 7 June 1692 an earthquake triggered a tsunami, and the pirate town was washed into the sea.

Pavlopetri

People started building the town of Pavlopetri in Greece 5,000 years ago, and lived there for two millenia. However, around 1000 BCE an earthquake shook the foundations of the town, lowering it into the sea. You can still see Pavlopetri lying beneath the waves today!

Doggerland

Today Britain is an island, but it wasn't always the case. For most of prehistory it was connected to Europe by a stretch of land called Doggerland (though there weren't any poodles there at the time). As the Ice Age ended and sea levels started to rise, Doggerland began to disappear. By 6500 BCE, Britain was all at sea.

Global warming

It's important to remember that disasters aren't just the stuff of history books. Due to global warming ice is once again melting and sea levels are rising. We must look after the environment, or more civilisations will be lost to the ocean.

THE CITY AT THE BOTTOM OF THE OCEAN

SPLASH! A team of divers rolled over the side of a boat, 3.5 miles (6 km) off the coast of Egypt. Deeper and deeper they dived, through murky waters and past curious fish, until they reached the seabed. The lead diver, Franck Goddio, is an underwater archaeologist. He was looking for something incredible hiding beneath the waves – not gold or buried treasure, but **Thonis-Heracleion**, the lost port city of ancient Egypt.

As the divers reached the bottom a giant human shape emerged from the darkness. It was a huge statue of an Egyptian pharaoh! Franck knew he had found the lost ancient city at last.

For 1,600 years Thonis-Heracleion was one of Egypt's most important towns. Situated on several small islands at the edge of the Nile delta, where the great river met the sea, it was home to thousands of people from all over the ancient world.

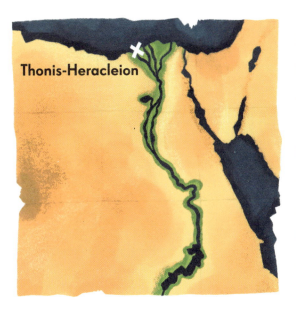

Thonis-Heracleion

Egyptian pharaohs had built lavish monuments throughout the city. As Franck and his team swam around they came across more and more treasures. There were startling discoveries – the statue of the Egyptian pharaoh was chiselled out of red granite, one of the hardest stones in the world. Pharaohs spent huge sums of money building statues in their honour. Imagine spending all that time carving a monument, only for it to sink in the sea.

Sticking out of the sand was a **large black stele**. A stele was basically a massive message board. In ancient times there were no newspapers, no TV, no internet, no post – no easy way to communicate at all. So how would anyone know what the king wanted them to do? Well, Egyptian pharaohs carved steles, big messages on big pieces of rock. Things like: *don't steal your neighbour's chickens*, *don't forget to pay your taxes*, and *the king is handsome and smart and everyone loves him*. The stele found at Thonis was carved in around 370 BCE by the pharaoh Nectanebo I. It let merchants know they had to pay a 10% tax to the temple of the goddess Neith.

Not all the finds were this big though. Underneath the corner of one of Thonis-Heracleion's main temples, archaeologists found **tiny statues of gods**, jewellery, and food. What were all of these things doing buried under a temple? Egyptians believed that you had to make offerings to the gods to prevent bad things from happening. They placed gifts under these buildings in the hope that the gods would stop them from falling down.

In its heyday Thonis-Heracleion was a town full of people and bustling markets. For hundreds of years a huge statue of Hapy, goddess of the Nile, stood guard over the city. So how did it all end up at the bottom of the sea? Scientists think it was a combination of nature, bad luck, and human ambition.

Thonis-Heracleion was built on top of **several islands** made of nothing but sand. This made it a perfect place for a port, as the water went right up to people's houses and the markets. However, the water was slowly destroying the town. Sand is not very strong, and easily absorbs water. It seems that little by little, year by year, Thonis-Heracleion was sinking into the sea.

This wasn't helped by the fact that Egypt is on the edge of a tectonic plate. You see, Europe and Africa are not sitting on the same piece of rock. They're actually very slowly crashing into each other. All of a sudden the rocks can slip, causing an earthquake. When this happened, Thonis would sink further into the sea.

The final nail in the coffin was the **ambition of the pharaohs**. On top of everything else, the last thing this town needed was for Egyptians to build large temples, palaces, and markets. But that's exactly what they did! Each new statue of a king slowly pushed the sand further into the sea. The Egyptians didn't know this, of course, but it's an important lesson to learn. It's always better to work with nature than against it.

If it wasn't for Franck and his team we might never know any of this. It wasn't by luck that he found the city, either. His boat was equipped with the latest technology – sonar that directed sound waves at the sea floor and equipment that measured the magnetism of what was below. Both of these tools were fired underneath the boat and Franck's team could see what bounced back up. What else might we find under the sea using such tools?

THE MIGHT OF THE
ROMAN EMPIRE

The Roman Empire has probably had more influence on European politics and culture than anything else. From its founding in 27 BCE, when Augustus Caesar declared himself emperor, to its final fall in 1453 CE, the empire was always changing and evolving.

The emperor

The empire was led by the Roman emperor. He had almost unlimited power over his subjects. Some emperors, such as Marcus Aurelius, were great rulers, but others used their power in horrible ways. The dreaded Caligula was such a terrible emperor that he was murdered by his own soldiers only four years into his reign!

Legions

The backbone of the Roman army was its legions. Each legion had around 6,000 soldiers. They wore heavy armour and held large shields, which they held in a tortoise formation in battles.

Absolutely minted

The Romans took coins with them everywhere they went. Each emperor minted new ones with his face on them, which archaeologists can use to date Roman sites.

Vast empire

At the height of its power the Roman Empire reached from the cold hills of Scotland in northern Europe to the Sahara desert in Africa. However in 476 CE the empire fell in the west of Europe, and by 1453 CE the empire only really controlled Constantinople (modern-day Istanbul, in Turkey) in the east.

Aqueducts

Romans loved bathing, and their cities often had sewer systems and public toilets. To bring enough water to the cities they built huge aqueducts across the empire. Many still work, 2,000 years later!

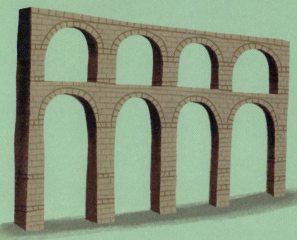

Different roles

Women in the Roman Empire could not be elected to government roles. However, some women advised emperors, while others ran successful businesses. Many women also chose to become priestesses, worshipping the many Roman gods.

Gladiator battles

Gladiator fights were a common feature of life in the early Roman Empire. Slaves would fight each other and wild animals, sometimes to the death! Successful gladiators were the celebrities of their time, like sports stars today.

Priestess of the goddess Vesta

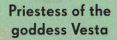

IN THE SHADOW OF THE VOLCANO

In the year 79 CE, the people of Pompeii were going about their daily lives. The markets were full of fresh fish caught that morning. Bakers baked bread for hungry customers. Farmers made wine in the countryside, stomping grapes between their toes. It was a typical day in the Roman Empire, the ancient superpower that spanned Europe and the Mediterranean. The citizens of Pompeii had no idea that their whole town would soon be destroyed, though a few residents might have noticed some suspicious warning signs. A small earthquake had rocked Pompeii a few weeks earlier, and wells across the town had gone dry. They might have wondered if these strange events had anything to do with Mount Vesuvius, the volcano that stood menancingly over the town.

BOOOM! KRraackkghgkkck! Vesuvius erupted, shaking the earth like a bowl of jelly! Glasses and pottery smashed, cats and dogs hid under tables and stairs, and people were thrown to the ground.

Huge clouds of ash were sent roaring into the sky, turning it black. The Romans said the explosion looked like a giant tree. Rocks came flying through the air as fast as missiles, smashing into the houses of Pompeii, knocking down walls and statues. But worse was to come. A massive avalanche of rocks, ash, and hot gas was pouring down Vesuvius. When it reached the town it covered everything in the deadly snow. Houses, restaurants, animals, people – *everything*. Those who were lucky escaped on boats at the harbour. As they looked back at the raging volcano, they saw their town in ruins, vanishing before their eyes. It would be almost 2,000 years before anyone would see Pompeii again.

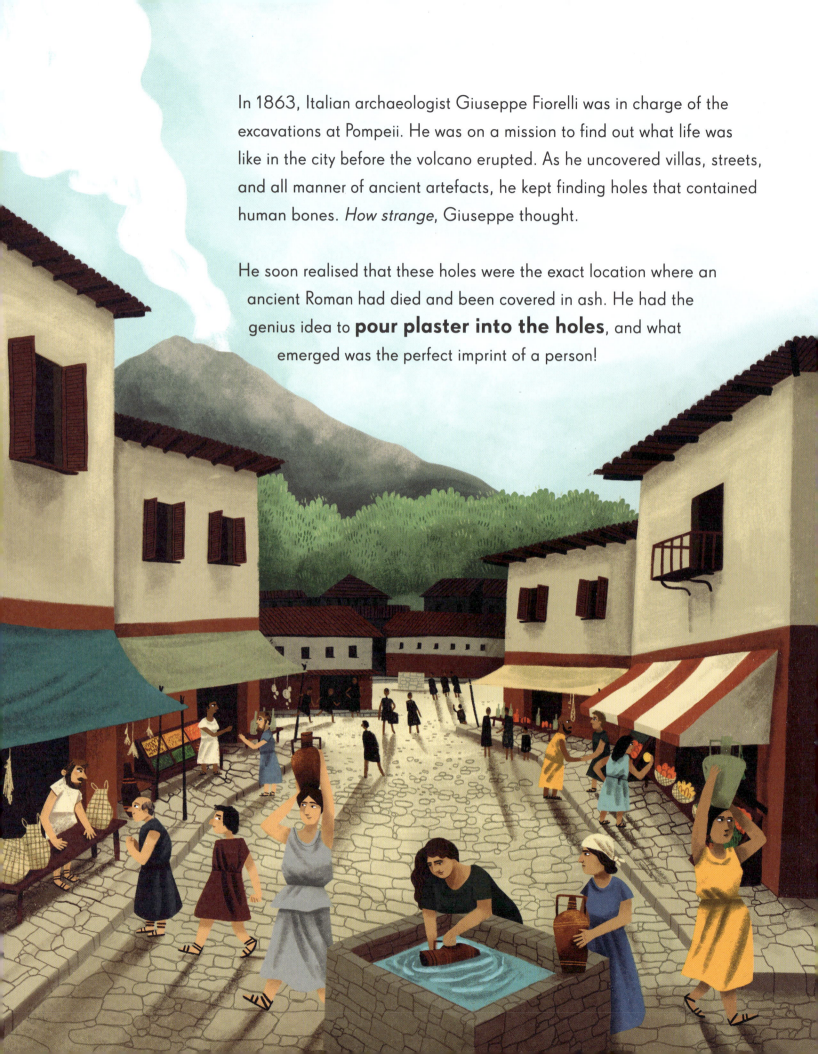

In 1863, Italian archaeologist Giuseppe Fiorelli was in charge of the excavations at Pompeii. He was on a mission to find out what life was like in the city before the volcano erupted. As he uncovered villas, streets, and all manner of ancient artefacts, he kept finding holes that contained human bones. *How strange*, Giuseppe thought.

He soon realised that these holes were the exact location where an ancient Roman had died and been covered in ash. He had the genius idea to **pour plaster into the holes**, and what emerged was the perfect imprint of a person!

Now if you visit Pompeii you can find many of these casts throughout the city. It's quite sad to think of all the people that died, but it is also the only place in the world where you can come face to face with **real ancient Romans**.

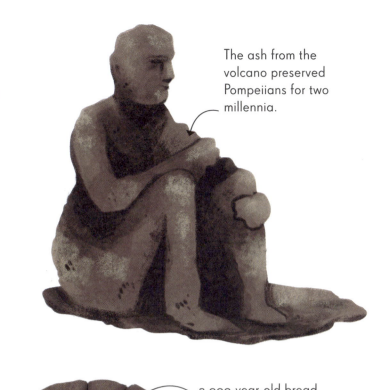

The ash from the volcano preserved Pompeiians for two millennia.

It's not just the bodies they found that make Pompeii such a special site. Lavish houses and streetside restaurants have been found with colourful paintings on the wall. Delicious round loaves of bread have been unearthed that were divided into eight pieces, as well as eggs with their shells intact. Archaeologists also discovered huge bronze gladiator helmets that protected fierce warriors while they were in combat.

2,000-year-old bread probably won't make nice toast.

They even found **public toilets with 20 seats in a row**, and no walls between them. You and all your friends could sit down and have a poo together. Romans would even share the same brush to wipe their bum! Walls of a few of the buildings were covered in graffiti: some of it friendly, some of it funny, some of it really mean. The graffiti has even given archaeologists a clue to when Vesuvius erupted – probably some time in October.

It's no exaggeration to say that Pompeii is one of the most extraordinary archaeological sites in the entire world. Nowhere else can provide us with so much information about life in the ancient world.

This Roman graffiti says "Gaius Pumidius Dipilus Was Here".

C PUMIDIUS DIPILUS HEIC FUIT

THE WARRIOR OF BOVER

The Caucasus Mountains, nestled between Europe and Asia, used to be a violent and wild frontier. In this area two worlds collided: the world of settled farming towns and the world of the grassy plains, or steppe, where nomadic people roamed on horseback. The kingdoms here were almost always at war, fighting off nomadic raiders that sought to plunder their towns. As a result societies, like the Kingdom of Urartu, prepared everyone for war – men and women alike.

Exciting tales of the **female warriors** are recorded in local stories such as the Nart sagas, in which women were said to be able to "cut out an enemy's heart with their swift, sharp swords". The ancient Greeks also had tales of female warriors from this region, called Amazonians, who mastered martial arts.

These epic sagas and legends were in Armenian archaeologist Anahit Khudaverdyan's mind when she started examining the remains of a woman's skeleton

from a graveyard site in the region called Bover 1. She wondered if they belonged to an ancient warrior. How could she tell just from the bones?

The first move was to date them. This woman, who the archaeologists called N 17, died around the year 700 BCE, during the time of the **Kingdom of Urartu**. So she definitely lived at the right time. Anahit looked at the bones more closely. If you exercise very hard, you will develop lots of strong muscles. These muscles leave marks on the bones where they're connected to them. From these marks Anahit could tell that N 17 was a very strong woman, particularly in the chest and shoulders. These are the muscles she would use to pull a bow back. The bow was perhaps the most important weapon of the day, especially for mounted archers.

Finally Anahit could see injuries on N 17. At one point she had been shot in the leg. It didn't kill her because the bones healed around the arrow, but for the rest of her life she had an arrow in her. She also probably died from a wound on her hip, perhaps from some sort of sword. Putting all these pieces together, it is likely that N 17 was a warrior!

THE TROPHIES OF THE CELTS

Thousands of years ago in **Gaul** (that's what the Romans called France) warfare was common. Different Celt chiefs vied for power and sometimes tribes would join together to raid the Greek colonies in southern Gaul. In 390 BCE a Gaulish king named Brennus even captured Rome! The Celts were well known for many things, including their metalwork, blue body paint, and mysterious druids. But they're probably most famous for their ferocious – and sometimes naked – sword-wielding warriors.

As a result of all this war, the Celts collected trophies to show everyone how tough they were. The most gruesome trophies of all were **human heads**.

Greek and Roman authors describe some of the gory Gaulish practices at the time. Apparently the Celts would tie the heads of defeated enemies to their horses. They would also cover the heads in a substance from **pine trees**, called resin, to preserve them. That way they could bring them out at special occasions for everyone to gawk at. Imagine being a kid back then? Instead of going to the cinema, you go to the town square to look at some fresh heads!

One problem, though, is that we sometimes don't know if the Romans and Greeks were exaggerating to make their enemies look bad, or whether the Celts really did this. To answer this question Salma Ghezal and a team of scientists from France analysed the remains of ancient skulls found at Celtic sites. Pine resin is very, very, VERY sticky. So even though it had been 2,000 years, on fragments from 11 different skulls the team found the tiny microscopic residue of pine resin!

So it seems the Greeks and Romans were not exaggerating. If you angered a Celt, you had better watch out – or else your sticky head might end up on someone's mantelpiece.

THE REIGN OF HORSES

The Mongolians are perhaps the greatest horse riders in history. The Asian steppe they call home is an ocean of swaying grass that stretches for 5,000 miles (8,000 km) – absolute heaven for horses. Famous leaders, like **Genghis Khan**, organised the nomadic horse-riding Mongolians into the most formidable army in history. These mighty soldiers travelled night and day across the wild lands, sleeping in round tents called yurts and conquering all who stood in their way. Considering the horse was so central to their way of life, it begs the question: when did Mongolians learn to ride horses?

How could we find evidence of horse riding in the archaeological record? Well it's here we run into a problem. We could excavate saddles or pictures of people riding horses, this would be clear evidence of riding. The problem is that delicate objects, such as saddles, don't tend to survive for very long in the ground. They quickly become nothing but mud and **worm food**.

Damaged jaw

Evidence of a bad back

Marks on teeth

In an attempt to solve the problem, archaeologists William Timothy Treal Taylor, Bayarsaikhan Jamsranjav, and Tuvshinjargal Tumurbaatar set out to find evidence of horse riding on the bones of horses themselves. Horse riding can be quite tough on horses (how would you like to carry around someone on your back?), and there are several key signs we can identify on their bones.

The excavated horse might have evidence of a bad back. Carrying a Mongolian warrior can be quite tough, especially if they had a lot for dinner, and the horse's skeleton would bear the brunt. Secondly, the reins used around a horse's mouth can leave telltale marks on their teeth and jaws.

With this in mind, the team looked at the skeletons of horses belonging to the **Khirigsuur culture** of Mongolia. They found clear signs of riding on them. This means that the people of Mongolia have been riding horses for at least 3,000 years!

THE SCIENCE AND MATHS OF
ANCIENT GREECE

Science and maths are responsible for the world around us. The phone in your pocket, the computer in your home, and the freezer in your kitchen that keeps your delicious ice cream perfectly cold – these are all a result of scientific experiments. We tend to think of science as being a very modern thing, but people in the ancient world were incredibly smart too! One civilisation that had a big impact on science was ancient Greece.

Flame-thrower

In the year 672 CE naval warfare changed forever. The Greeks developed a flame-thrower to burn their enemies' wooden boats! We're not sure of the exact chemical recipe but it could even burn on the water, making it a deadly threat.

Steam engine

In 100 BCE, Hero of Alexandria developed a working steam engine! A cauldron of water would be placed above a fire. As the water heated up it shot out steam, spinning the machine.

Hippocrates

Hippocrates was the father of modern medicine. He was one of the first people to understand that disease was caused by problems within the body, not angry gods. He realised that through observation we could understand and treat illnesses. His oath "to do no harm" is still repeated by doctors today.

All aboard

As you can see on this map, one area of Greece is very narrow. The city of Corinth realised they could build a boat track across Greece, connecting two seas and saving sailors a lot of time. This track was called the Diolkos and in a way it was the world's first railway!

Diolkos

Pythagoras

Pythagoras lived around the year 500 BCE and is most famous for working out a formula for discovering the area of a triangle. This might sound a bit boring, but it was actually a huge discovery. Everytime you drive across a bridge without it collapsing, thank Pythagoras!

THE ANCIENT COMPUTER

In the year 1900 sponge divers (yup, those guys again), were diving off the Greek island of Antikythera when they discovered a shipwreck that had been lying peacefully under the waves for 2,000 years. Inside the wreck they found incredible ancient artefacts, such as life-size bronze statues and a huge head of the philosopher Philitas of Cos. However the most incredible discovery was an unassuming lump of corroded metal. As the device was cleaned it became apparent that it was a unique and mysterious find. This is the story of the **Antikythera Mechanism**, in a way the world's first computer.

Now this was not a computer in the modern sense. It couldn't play any games, you couldn't watch videos of funny dogs on it, or do your homework. Its exact function was not understood in 1900. It wasn't until the 1970s that X-ray results first revealed what it did, and not until 2006 that we fully understood what was going on inside this funky piece of metal.

The Antikythera Mechanism was a device for calculating the **positions of the planets** and bodies in the Solar System, or at least the ones that are visible to the naked eye: the Sun, the Moon, Mercury, Venus, Mars, Jupiter, and Saturn.

It's probably easier to imagine it as **a type of clock**. Originally a small wooden box would have contained the different cogs and gears. With the turning of one dial on the side of the mechanism you could see the position of all of the celestial bodies at the same time. It may have been used to calculate the correct date to hold the Olympic Games.

Historians had heard of such devices – old Roman and Greek texts mention them – but they weren't 100% sure if they truly existed or exactly how they worked. Until those sponge divers found the Antikythera wreck, we had never ever seen one! It really is a fantastic testament to the scientific talents of the ancient Greeks. Not only could they calculate the movements of the planets without telescopes, but they could also produce cogs and dials accurate enough to reproduce these movements in one convenient box. Genius!

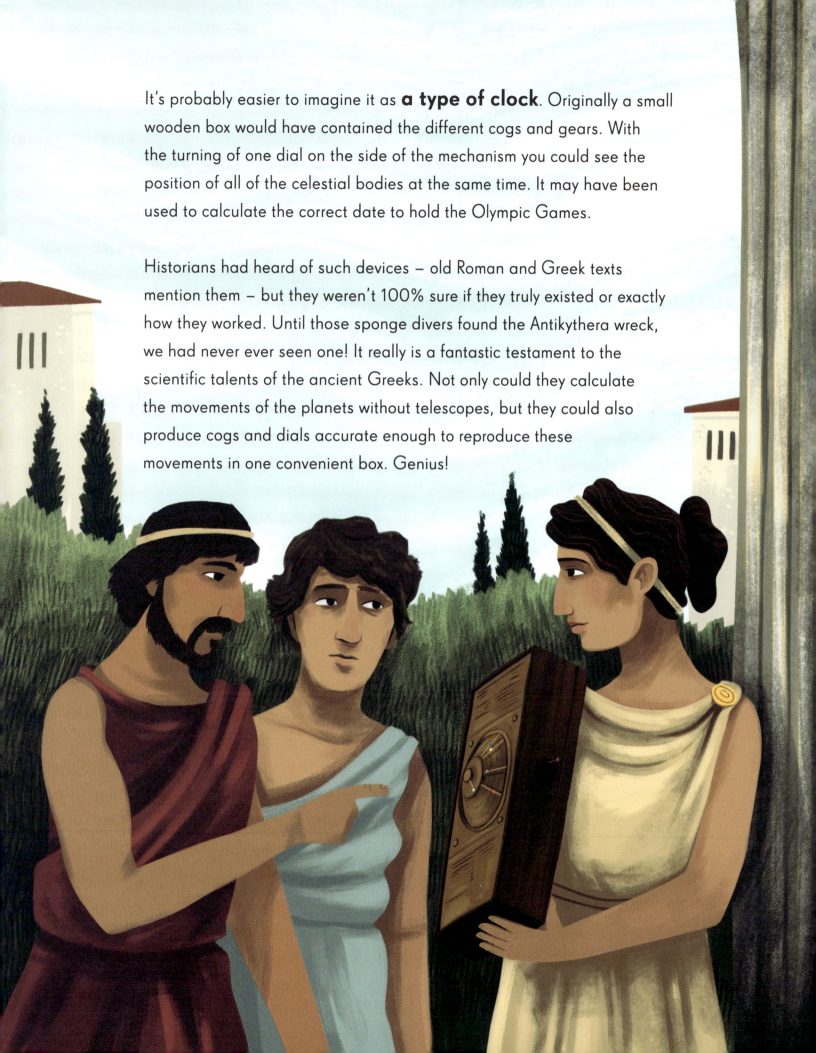

THE WORSHIPPING OF
ANIMAL GODS

Some animals are fast, some can fly, some are strong, and some are kind of creepy – it's fair to say the animal kingdom is full of wonders! With so many incredible creatures around it's no surprise that animal gods and spirits feature prominently in both ancient and modern beliefs.

Rainbow serpent

Some Aboriginal groups in Australia believe that a rainbow serpent emerged from the water to create the mountains and carve rivers. Many pieces of ancient Aboriginal artwork feature the story of this slithering creator.

Nāga

In Hinduism, Buddhism, and Jainism, the half-human, half-cobra Nāga live in an underground kingdom. It is said they only bite the truly evil or those that are destined to die young.

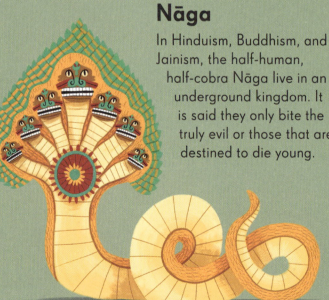

Sobek

Sobek was the Egyptian god of death and burial. At the temple in Fayum a crocodile was kept as the representative of the god and was even mummified when it died!

Shark god

Ebisu is one of Japan's seven fortunate gods. He is often depicted carrying a rod, or as a whale shark. Ebisu protects fishermen and brings in huge catches of fish.

Minotaur

The Minotaur was a mythical creature from ancient Greece with the body of a man and the head of a bull. He lived in the centre of a dizzying labyrinth and was fed children!

Dragons

In both Europe and Asia ancient legends tell of fearsome dragons. In Europe they can fly and breathe fire. In Asia, they don't have wings and are associated with water and good luck.

Ravens

Odin is a powerful god in Norse mythology. He has two ravens, Huginn and Muninn, who fly around the world bringing him information. If you ever think a raven is following you, watch out, it could be one of Odin's spies!

Ganesh

Ganesh is an elephant-headed god in Hinduism. He is known to remove obstacles. People often pray to him before they begin anything new, just to make sure things go smoothly.

THE LEGEND OF THE GIANT SNAKE

In amongst the fields and woods of Ohio sits one of North America's most mysterious ancient monuments. It's something you can't find anywhere else in the entire world – a snake 400 m (1,300 ft) long!

The first question archaeologists usually like to answer when confronted with an artefact like this is when was it made? This could tell us a lot about an object's construction, but unfortunately, it's not always so simple. Two different teams excavated portions of **Serpent Mound** and came back with two different results! One team found that it was built around 300 BCE by the Adena culture. The second team found that it was built around the year 1070 CE, and so must have been built by the Fort Ancient culture.

How can we explain this? How can people a thousand years apart have built the same monument? There are two possible explanations.

The first is that one of the teams was wrong, which happens all the time in archaeology. It's not easy to reconstruct the past! The second explanation is that the giant serpent was first built in 300 BCE, but then repaired or added to in 1070 CE.

Why build a giant snake in the first place (other than the fact that it is very cool)? It could have been some sort of calendar. The head aligns with the Sun at the summer solstice – the longest day in the year – and the tail with the winter solstice. As we saw in the Neolithic period, working out the correct time of year was extremely important for ancient farmers.

What about the giant disc the snake is eating? We're not 100% sure what it represents, but intriguingly, around the year 1070 CE, **Halley's Comet** flew past the Earth. Perhaps during the repair work, these ancient architects chose to add a representation of the mysterious light that was shooting across their night sky. How cool is that?

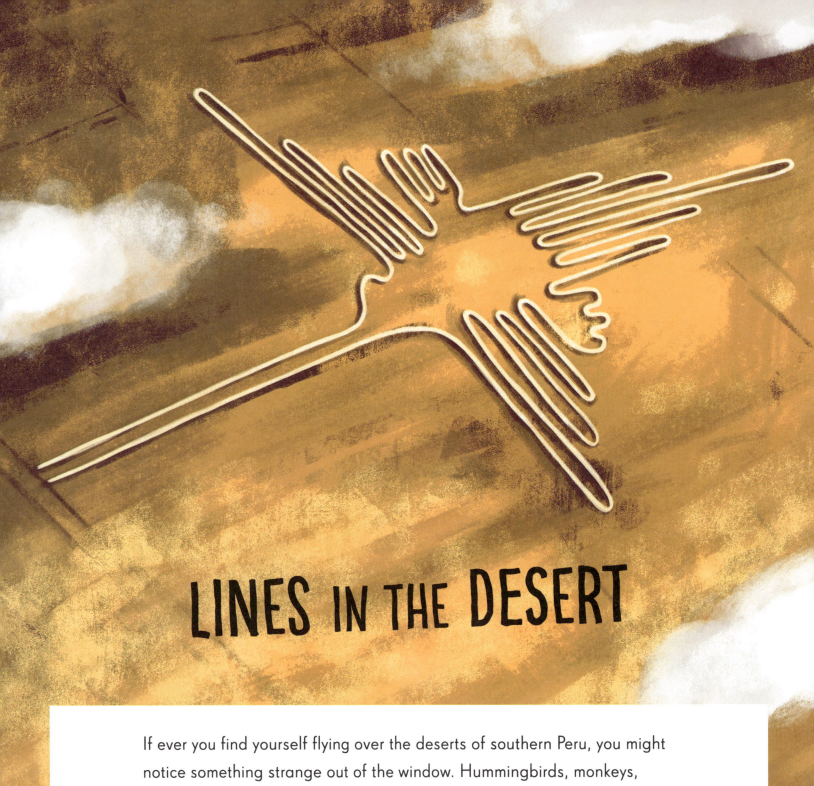

LINES IN THE DESERT

If ever you find yourself flying over the deserts of southern Peru, you might notice something strange out of the window. Hummingbirds, monkeys, spiders – a vast assortment of **wild animals** scratched into the desert rocks below. And they're HUGE. The hummingbird you're looking at right now is almost 100 m (330 ft) long! All of these magnificent creatures were created by the Nazca, a desert people that lived in southern Peru about 2,000 years ago.

The Nazca were incredible engineers. By building sophisticated wells, called *puquios*, they were able to turn their dry and dusty home into an abundant garden to support their families. The Nazca didn't just use their engineering skills for agriculture though, they also created these gigantic images across the desert. In terms of construction, the **Nazca Lines** are very simple. Rocks and earth were moved to one side to create these big images – they're only about 10–15 cm (4–6 in) deep. The Nazca couldn't fly up into the air to see their masterpieces as they made them, they had to create all of these images just by measuring their position. It would have been really hard! What were the lines for? We're not sure.

Thanks to modern technology though, archaeologists and their **drones** can fly like hummingbirds across Peru's vast southern desert to find out more about the mysterious lines. A team of archaeologists from Yamagata University in Japan, led by Masato Sakai, have discovered over 200 more images this way, and estimate there may be over a thousand still to find! As the lines are so subtle, computers and drones are able to find them much more easily than the human eye. One recent discovery wouldn't be out of place in a cartoon: a figure wearing some kind of hat and wielding a bat. Who they were, we can only imagine!

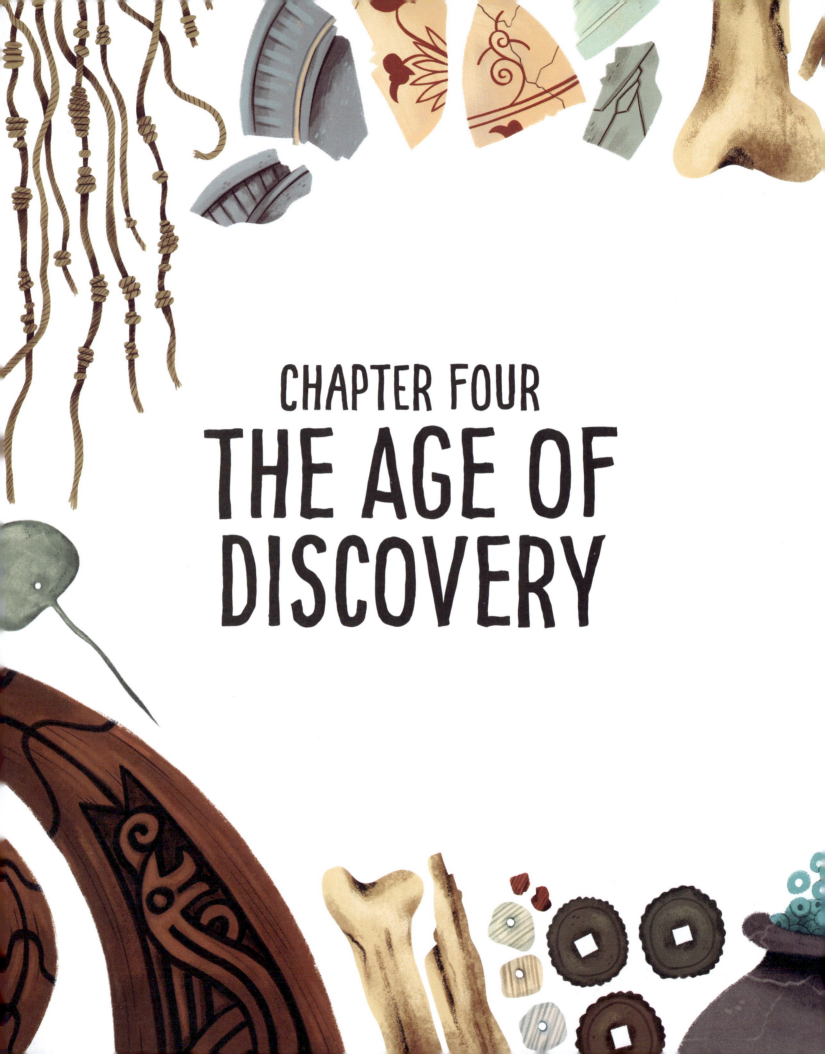

CHAPTER FOUR
THE AGE OF DISCOVERY

Our final adventures are the most adventurous of them all! This chapter begins a smidge over 1,000 years ago. The Vikings were sailing the North Atlantic, leaving behind some pretty smelly clues. The Polynesians were navigating the Pacific Ocean, reaching far-flung islands. And one of the greatest sailors of all time was setting off from China in his giant treasure fleet.

THE MOUND OF SURPRISES

The first thing to appear as archaeologists dug down into the grassy mound was the unmistakable **green tint of bronze** that had been long buried. The team from the National Museum of Korea were excavating Tomb 120 in Gyeongju, the ancient capital city of Korea's Silla kingdom. What they had just found was a bronze shoe. "Bronze shoe? Can't be comfy!", I hear you say. You're right – but these shoes weren't made to be worn, they were offerings to be placed in the tombs of Silla nobility.

The most famous artefacts to ever be found at Gyeongju were **tall gold crowns** decorated with green jade. They were worn by the Silla kings sometime in the years 400 CE to 600 CE – the crown jewels of ancient Korea. These were found in the early 20th century, but Korean archaeologists had decided to dig in some of the tombs again, which is why they found themselves looking at the bronze shoe.

Why would archaeologists excavate the same tomb twice? Well, in the past archaeologists didn't have the same technology we do now, and to be honest they were often just focused on finding treasure, not understanding history (remember the guy who blew up the Nubian pyramids?). So archaeologists frequently go back and reassess what was found before with new tools and an open mind.

It was just as well they went back. Outside the tomb they found huge piles of jars. One contained 7,700 animal bones! These were probably left at a later date by people wanting to remember those buried in the tomb. What's interesting is that these rituals were never written down, and weren't discovered by the first excavation. It turns out that in ancient Silla, people commemorated the dead in exquisite style. Inside the jars were the remains of really expensive foods like sea urchin, dolphin, and even **pufferfish** – a fish so poisonous that if it's not prepared correctly, whoever eats it will end up in a tomb themselves!

THE AGE OF
THE VIKINGS

Today, the Vikings are remembered as the fiercest of fierce warriors. Sea-faring raiders from Scandinavia with their hearts set on stealing your gold, burning your church, and giving you a good bop on the nose. While this may be true, Vikings were so much more than that. They were also poets, traders, farmers, and explorers. The Viking age lasted from about 700 CE to 1100 CE.

Runes

The Vikings had an alphabet made up of letters called runes, which they cut into stone or wood to commemorate important events, or sometimes just to say things like, "Haermund Hardaxe carved these runes".

The Viking world

The Vikings were amazing explorers. From their home in Scandinavia they sailed as far as North America in the west and Iraq in the east.

God of thunder

Thor was the Viking god of thunder and defender of Asgard, the realm of the gods. With his mighty hammer, Mjolnir, he fought a snake so big it wrapped around the entire world!

Normal people

The word "Viking" means a raider – it was a job description. But not all Vikings raided. Most of the time they were farmers, not fighters, and they loved to sing epic poetry! Viking women weren't just stuck at home either – they could become successful businesswomen.

Fun and games

Vikings loved games and tricks. In Scotland, a large collection of chess pieces was discovered. The one on the left might be biting its shield as a sign of ferociousness!

Ships and trading

The Vikings sailed the world in incredible longships, crossing oceans and going up rivers. There weren't any rooms though, so it could get cold on board! They would trade goods – such as jewellery, amber, and even seal fat – with people across Europe and parts of Asia.

THE BURIED VIKING SHIP

According to legend, in 1870 a farmer from Oseberg called Johannes Hansen left his home in Norway and sailed to America seeking his fortune. One night he met a **fortune teller** who told him, "Return to Norway. There are treasures enough on your farm. Just dig below the hill". Johannes had no idea how right the fortune teller was. He ignored the suggestion and sold the farm.

Thirty years later, in 1904, archaeologist Gabriel Gustafson started excavating the hill as it was in danger of being destroyed by treasure hunters. As his team dug down they found a curved piece of wood. Incredibly, this was the prow of a Viking ship! Gustafson knew this could mean only one thing: beneath this hill an extremely important Viking was buried!

The archaeologists dug down further, eventually revealing an entire ship. On board was absolutely everything a Viking would need to enjoy the afterlife: bed, treasure chest, intricately-carved wagon, expensive boots, farm tools, 15 horses, 6 dogs, 2 cows, and even 3 sleighs (because even when you're dead, sledging is great fun). But who was buried in it?

In the centre of the boat lay **two women**, one about 70 years old, the other about 50. In Viking society women could become rich and powerful – it's even possible that the older woman buried in the boat was a mysterious Norwegian Queen named Asa. We may never know for sure, but it's fun to daydream!

A STINK AT THE BANK

Just to warn you here, this story is not for the faint of heart! In 1972, Lloyds Bank wanted to build a new branch in the centre of **York**, in the UK. It is a very historic area of the city, full of charming timber-frame buildings and a huge medieval cathedral. Archaeologists were called in to do a survey before construction could begin. As they dug down they uncovered extremely old wooden planks. They had reached Viking York, or as the Vikings called it, Jorvik!

So many incredible finds were unearthed, including hundreds of thousands of pieces of pottery and Viking houses – enough finds to open a museum. But by far the most intriguing (and stinkiest), was a preserved Viking poo!

In archaeology, a preserved poo is known as a **coprolite**. This medieval chocolate log was an absolute belter, 20 cm (8 in) long! Obviously this is a very funny discovery, and you might think the archaeologists were unhappy to find it, but nothing could be further from the truth. Archaeologists can actually learn a lot from this brown gold.

Because it's a natural substance, poo can be dated, allowing archaeologists to figure out the age of the site they're working on. It can also tell us a lot about ancient diets. The individual who deposited this poo enjoyed eating a lot of meat and bread but not so many vegetables. It can also tell us about the health of people at the time. The Lloyds Bank coprolite contained hundreds of tiny **microscopic eggs**, belonging to worms that can live inside your body. Having worms inside you probably won't cause any major health problems but it can be painful when they leave your body. They can emerge from any hole, even the corner of your eye! Infestations like this were a regular problem for our ancestors in times when clean drinking water was hard to come by.

Who knew we could learn so much from this ancient bank deposit!

Scientist studying the coprolite

EXPLORERS OF
THE PACIFIC

The Polynesians are the greatest maritime civilisation in human history. No people have made the ocean their home quite like them. From New Zealand in the south to Hawaii in the north, the Polynesians are the original explorers of the Pacific Ocean – which takes up an incredible one-third of the entire world!

Canoe life

Between the 1100s and 1200s the Polynesians travelled between their island homes on large double-hulled voyaging canoes. These were big enough to carry whole families as well as enough food and water for the journey. Polynesian sailors were experts at navigating by the stars and could even read the ocean currents.

Sea world

Apart from New Zealand, Polynesians mostly live on hundreds of small Pacific islands. Some are close together, but many are extremely remote! The Polynesian triangle is marked by Hawaii in the north, New Zealand in the southwest, and Easter Island in the southeast. Each island has its own unique interpretation of Polynesian culture.

Journey snacks

Food is important for any long journey at sea. The most important foods for Polynesian sailors were yams, sweet potatoes, and pigs. The yams and potatoes could be turned into a fermented food called *poi*, which would keep fresh for the whole trip.

Yam

Sweet potato

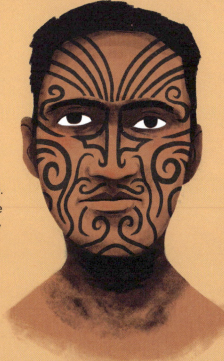

Tattoos

For many Polynesian people, tattoos are an important part of their identity. The Maori of New Zealand call tattoos *moko*. Many of their designs represent a unique aspect of that person's life or their family history. Originally they were chiselled onto the face using an *uhi* (albatross bone), and the coloured pigment was made from fat and charcoal.

THE WATCHMEN OF RAPA NUI

On the Polynesian island of Rapa Nui, also known as Easter Island, are some of the most amazing and unique statues in world history. Standing guard over the island, with their backs to the sea, are the **moai**. The tallest moai is called Paro. It is almost 10 m (30 ft) tall and weighs as much as 50 cars!

There aren't just three or four of these colossal statues either, over 900 were carved! All on a small island with a tiny population. The people of Rapa Nui put a lot of effort into carving and moving these moai. Teams of craftsmen would carve them out of the side of a volcano in the Rano Raraku quarry.

One question that had been bothering archaeologists and historians for a long time was how the people of Rapa Nui moved the moai from the side of a volcano down to the beach.

The Rapa Nui people who lived on the island were asked what they thought had happened. **They said the statues walked down.** Archaeologists who weren't from the island scoffed at the idea. They presumed the moai were moved by a sledge, or maybe pushed on rollers, but each time they put it to the test, they failed.

Finally a team of archaeologists, including former Rapa Nui governor Sergio Rapu Haoa, tried walking the statues. They analysed moai still in the quarries, moai that had fallen by the side of the road, and moai that had made it to the shore. After an investigation they realised three teams of people could walk the moai down the road by carefully pulling on ropes. It just goes to show that archaeology works best when local knowledge is combined with scientific methods.

So why did the Rapa Nui spend all this time building moai? What did they mean to them? This is not an easy question to answer, but understanding how and why people do things is one of the most interesting parts of archaeology! The moai represented **notable ancestors** of the Rapa Nui people. Their society was organised by rank, and kings were viewed with great respect. A powerful king would have his followers carve a moai in his honour, and to honour his ancestors. Because of this the moai are like a historical record, going all the way back to the first kings and chiefs of Rapa Nui, like Hotu Matu'a, who first settled the island.

There was even an element of competition in moai-building. Rival kings would want to be seen building the biggest and most elaborate statues to impress their neighbours. Kings do love to brag! There may have been a very practical reason for constructing moai as well. One of the challenges of living on a small island is that it can be easy to run out of food. You don't have much land to grow on, and major storms can damage the crops you're growing.

Some unfinished moai remain in the volcano

As a result of this, the Rapa Nui were really excellent farmers. They built small rock gardens to trap nutrients for their plants and keep them safe from the wild, stormy weather of the south Pacific (nobody wants to eat a rotten sweet potato after all). The moai may have also helped in this process. One of the best places on the island to grow crops was on **the volcano of Rano Raraku,** the same place where the statues were quarried. Archaeologists and biologists dug up the soil there and looked inside it for ancient seeds and pollen. They found that Rano Raraku was full of sweet potatoes, gourds, bananas – everything the Rapa Nui loved to eat! It seems that the carving of moai created a lot of rock dust and powder, which made the soil excellent for growing food.

You could say the moai protected the Rapa Nui in two ways. Firstly they acted as guardians of the people, guiding them spiritually. Secondly they helped provide a nice cooked dinner with bananas for dessert!

Rock garden

THE GIGANTIC
INCA EMPIRE

Despite only numbering about 100,000 people, the Incas built the largest empire in the history of the Americas. It stretched 1,500 miles (2,500 km) from the humid jungles of Colombia, over the mountains of Peru, and through the dry deserts of Chile. Such a diverse empire created a fascinating civilisation.

South America

The Inca Empire dominated the west of South America. The Incas started expanding with the ascent of Pachacuti Inca Yupanqui ("Reverser of the World") to the Incan throne in 1438 CE.

Sensing a pattern

Incan textiles are world famous. The women best at weaving were called the *aclla*. They lived in the *acllawasi*, or "house of chosen women", and produced clothing for the army, the nobility, and the emperor.

Incan emperor

The Inca emperor was called the *Sapa Inca*. Living in the capital city Cuzco, he led a luxurious life: feasting, drinking from gold cups, and wearing the finest clothes and the *Mascaipacha* – the Incan crown.

Record keeping

The Incas organised their empire using *quipus*, or knot records. Each rope and knot meant something different. Some acted like an alphabet that could record history, while others were used to list supplies.

On the edge

The Incas were incredible farmers, despite many of them living high in the Andean Mountains. They built terraces to turn the inhospitable terrain into the perfect environment for their favourite food – potatoes. The land was divided amongst three groups: farms for the temples, farms for the king, and farms owned by regular people.

Roads

To move armies and goods the Incas built a huge road network. There was even a system of relay runners, called *chasquis*, that could communicate messages over long distances. These runners could send a message as far as 150 miles (240 km) in a single day!

THE MYSTERY OF
MACHU PICCHU

American explorer Hiram Bingham and his Peruvian guides, Melchor Arteaga and Sergeant Carrasco, had been hiking for hours. As they hacked through vegetation and crept along treacherous mountain paths, any wrong step could send them falling into the valley below. It was 1911 and they were searching for the last capital of the Inca Empire, but they came across something much more incredible – the city of Machu Picchu!

As they neared the top of the mountain they encountered a farmer, whose 11-year-old son Pablito said he knew the way to an ancient palace. Pablito led the group further up, along an Incan road. When they reached the top they couldn't believe their eyes. An entire **Incan palace** carved out of the top of the mountain!

Machu Picchu was built 600 years ago for Inca emperor Pachacutec and was probably his holiday home. It had everything an emperor would need: farms built on terraces for fresh food, a temple for the king to communicate with the gods, and most importantly peace and quiet! It was a remote location and was not easy to access. It was so hard to get to that the **Spanish invaders** who arrived in the 16th century didn't find it. This meant that when Hiram and Pablito appeared it was still mostly intact.

There were many incredible artefacts among the ruins, including silver *tupu*, pins that rich Incas used to fasten their clothes (you don't want your pants falling down up a big mountain). Hiram agreed with the Peruvian government that he could take these artefacts back to Yale University in the United States, where he worked, on the condition that when Peru asked for them back they would be returned. But Yale ended up keeping them for over 100 years! Eventually the artefacts were returned to Peru and the fabulous treasures of the Inca Empire are now home where they belong.

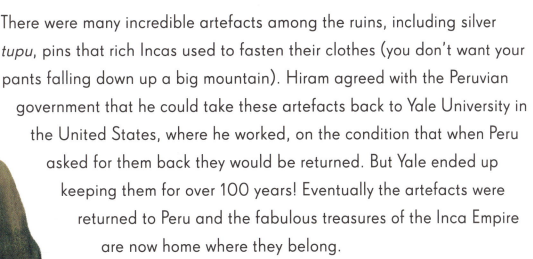

Silver tupu

THE DESTROYED INCAN IDOL

In 1533, the Spanish conquistador Hernando Pizarro was leaving Peru after conquering the Inca Empire. In his wake he left a country ruined by invasion, disease, and internal fighting. The Spanish were dedicated Catholics and they believed the religion of the Incas to be a sin. As a result the monuments and idols of the empire were destroyed. Pizarro thought one **Incan statue** in particular was pure devil worship. He ordered his men to "Undo the vault where the idol was and break him in front of everyone". The idol was thus lost to history, destroyed for good…

Fast forward to 1938 and American archaeologist Albert Giesecke was excavating a temple in the Incan town of Pachamac when he uncovered

a huge wooden statue. Each side was carved with intricate but mysterious faces. Was this the sculpture that Pizarro had destroyed? The one that the Incas believed had the power to see the future? "Surely not," people said. Some even accused Albert of faking the discovery.

Almost 100 years later, a team of scientists led by Chilean archaeologist Marcela Sepúlveda decided to get to the truth. It was quite a puzzle to unravel. The idol was apparently worshipped by the Incas, but it was in the earlier artistic style of the **Wari people**. They decided to date the wood, and the results were astounding. It came from a tree that lived around the year 800 CE! They also put the idol through a sophisticated X-ray scanner and found microscopic traces of paint, proof that it was once brightly coloured.

This means that not only was this the genuine idol, but that it had been worshipped by the people of the Andes for 700 years before the arrival of Pizarro. It seems that Pizarro either lied about destroying the idol, or his men didn't carry out the order. Fortunately for us, the incredible Pachacamac Idol survives to this day!

THE TREASURE OF THE SAMURAI

If you like to lead a quiet and peaceful life, then you probably wouldn't have enjoyed living in 15th-century Japan. The country was in the middle of a bloody civil war that would last 100 years. Lords called *daimyos* ruled their own territories and constantly fought each other to increase their power. If a *daimyo* was powerful enough, he might become *shogun*, overlord of all Japan (but still in theory under the emperor). Underneath the *daimyo* were the samurai, **Japan's warrior class**. In their fantastic armour they fought battles with razor-sharp swords, bows, and spears. Meanwhile ninjas would be dispatched in secret to assassinate political rivals.

All of this war and conflict resulted in a terrible amount of death and destruction, but it also caused practical problems, too. One of the biggest

being, *where do I put my money?* Nowadays we can put our hard-earned cash in a bank. Even if you have millions of pounds or precious diamonds, they'll be safe. If the bank is robbed, insurance will simply cover your losses. But none of these things existed in the age of the samurai in Japan. So how could you stop a **ninja** from stealing your money? There was only one option – bury it!

In 2018, the Japanese archaeologist Yoshiyuki Takise was excavating underneath the floor of a samurai's house near Tokyo when he unearthed a huge pot. Inside were copper coins, once shiny but now stained blue from being in the ground for 500 years. Not just one coin, or even a thousand, but **260,000 coins!** An absolutely huge amount of treasure.

This raises a ton of questions, but the two biggest are: how did this samurai get so rich, and why did he not come back for his money? What do you think?

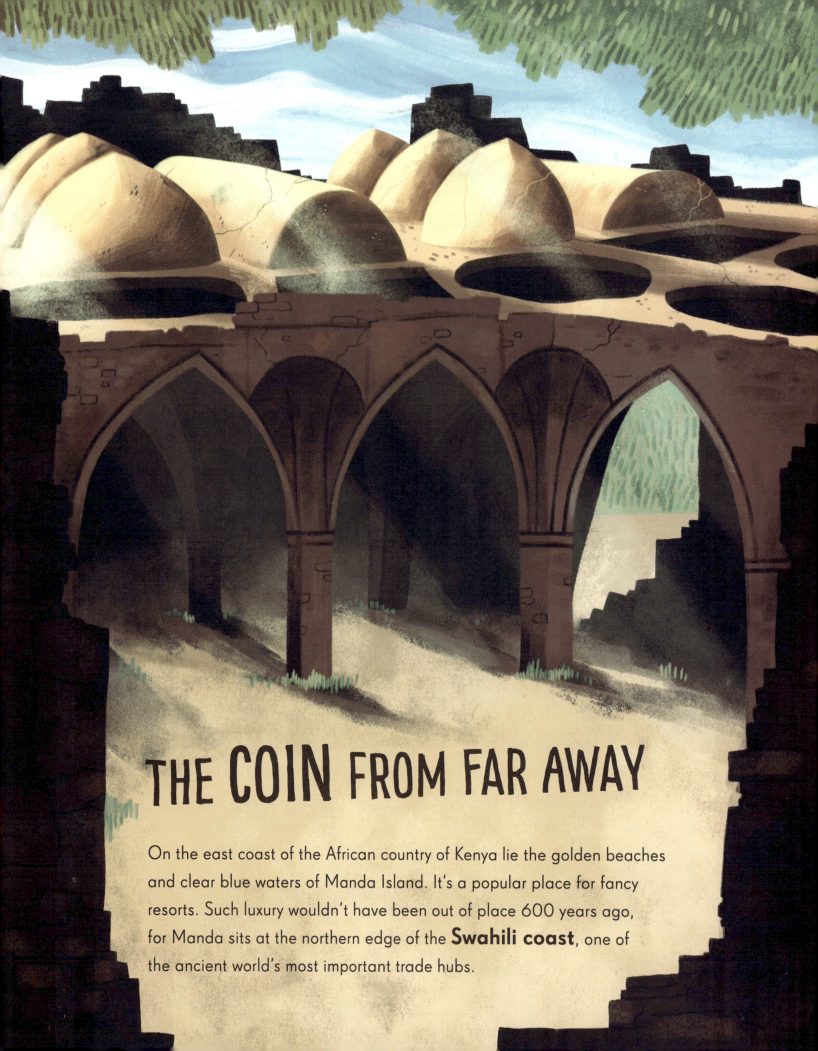

THE COIN FROM FAR AWAY

On the east coast of the African country of Kenya lie the golden beaches and clear blue waters of Manda Island. It's a popular place for fancy resorts. Such luxury wouldn't have been out of place 600 years ago, for Manda sits at the northern edge of the **Swahili coast**, one of the ancient world's most important trade hubs.

Broken pottery pieces

Starting around the year 600 CE and continuing into the 1500s, the Swahili people grew fabulously wealthy as the traders between two huge regions. They exchanged materials from Africa for the finest luxuries that Asia could produce, turning the Indian Ocean into a highway of ancient commerce. With this wealth they turned their small islands into majestic towns made from coral! You can still see many of these monuments today, such as the **Great Mosque of Kilwa Kisiwani** and its many coral domes. At home the traders showed off their wealth by displaying pottery that had come all the way from China.

On Manda in 2013, Dr Chapurukha Kusimba of Chicago's Field Museum was excavating a **midden**. A midden is the archaeological term for what is basically an ancient pile of rubbish. (You can find out a lot from what people throw away – I'm sure we could learn a lot about you from going through your bins!) As Chapurukha dug down, something shiny caught his eye: an old coin! Someone must have thrown it away by accident, and probably spent ages looking for it.

There was something particularly special about this coin, though. It wasn't made in Manda, nor in a neighbouring region like Arabia. It had come all the way from China! In fact, it may be a tiny piece of evidence for some of the greatest sea voyages of all time, those of the legendary **Zheng He**.

Why was this small coin, found in an ancient rubbish pit, evidence of a voyage? And who was Zheng He anyway?

Well, to answer these questions we have to start with when the coin was minted (the coin doesn't taste minty, that's just the word people use for making a coin). The small coin found by Chapurukha was minted by the **Chinese emperor Yongle**, who reigned between 1403 and 1425.

Emperor Yongle had decided to build a huge fleet to travel across the Indian Ocean to increase trade and, just for good measure, remind everyone how special and important the Chinese emperor was. The treasure fleet was going to be the largest in history – 317 ships, the largest of which were over 100 m (330 ft) long! Each one would be resplendent in red silk sails.

To command his fleet, Yongle selected Zheng He. Zheng was born with the name **Ma Ho** to a Muslim family in Yunnan, in southwest China. However when he was only ten years old he was captured by Yongle's army and forced to serve the emperor. Ma Ho was a good soldier and was known for having an incredibly loud, booming voice –useful for shouting across the water to his other ships. He rose through the ranks to become one of the emperor's most trusted men. The emperor even changed Ma's name to Zheng He.

Zheng He

Zheng set sail with his fleet of ships. He headed south, past what is now Vietnam, Thailand, and Malaysia, and across the ocean to India, before scooting around the Arabian Peninsula and sailing down into Africa. At each location Zheng's ships traded with the kingdoms of the ancient world, determined to bring back piles of treasure for the emperor. Zheng eventually went on **seven epic expeditions** and brought back creatures that wowed the emperor and his court, including giraffes! However the cost of the expeditions was too great, and after the seventh voyage the treasure fleet would not set sail again. But dotted around the Indian Ocean remain clues from the spectacular voyages, like the little coin found on Manda.

The voyages of Zheng He

THE WORLD OF THE
MISSISSIPPI

Nine hundred years ago in North America the Mississippian culture was thriving. Towns and cities sprang up along rivers, in particular the Mississippi. The corn-loving, game-playing, arrowhead-making Mississippians were an absolutely fascinating bunch. Let's see what makes their civilisation so interesting and try to decipher the ancient riddles they've left us.

Sense of community

The Mississippian world was centred around the city of Cahokia, though the civilisation was probably not controlled by Cahokia, but made up of different communities (the different coloured bits on the map) that all shared a common culture.

Water taxis

Canoes were an absolutely essential part of life for the Mississippians. In a world without roads, they were the fastest way to get around.

Female farmers

We can tell from figurines excavated at Cahokia that women played an important role as the farmers of society. Beans, maize (corn), squash, and nuts were the staples of this society and the farmers grew enough to support thousands of people!

Chunkey

The people of the Mississippi loved to play a game called *chunkey*. One player would roll a ceramic disc and other players would throw spears at it. Whoever got their spears closest to the disc was the winner!

Cahokia

The largest city on the Mississippi was Cahokia, which at its height was probably home to around 5,000 people. At the heart of the city was an enormous mound.

Arrowheads

The Cahokians were skilled at producing elaborate arrowheads. Each one was made from flint that was heated before being carefully shaped into points – often with serrations around the edge.

THE BIRDMAN OF CAHOKIA

In 1967, Melvin Fowler was examining mounds in the ancient North American city of **Cahokia**, just outside the city of St Louis in Missouri. As he was driving along one day, one of the mounds in particular caught his eye. Unlike all the other mounds at Cahokia, it wasn't square but a rectangle, and it didn't face north to south, but was offset at a slight angle. *How odd*, he thought. Melvin parked his car and pulled out his compass. He soon realised the mound was aligned to the summer and winter solstice, which – as we've discussed many times in this book – was significant to ancient farmers.

Melvin tried to find the mound on his map of Cahokia, but couldn't see it anywhere. This mound, which would later be called **Mound 72**, had been missed by the initial survey.

Melvin decided that his team of archaeologists needed to excavate as soon as possible. Many earlier mounds from Cahokia had been totally destroyed to make way for St Louis, and Melvin knew it was a race against time to find any **ancient artefacts**. He could not have anticipated what he would find though. Underneath the strange but unassuming Mound 72 was the most elaborate burial ever found in the history of North America…

Some mounds were blown up

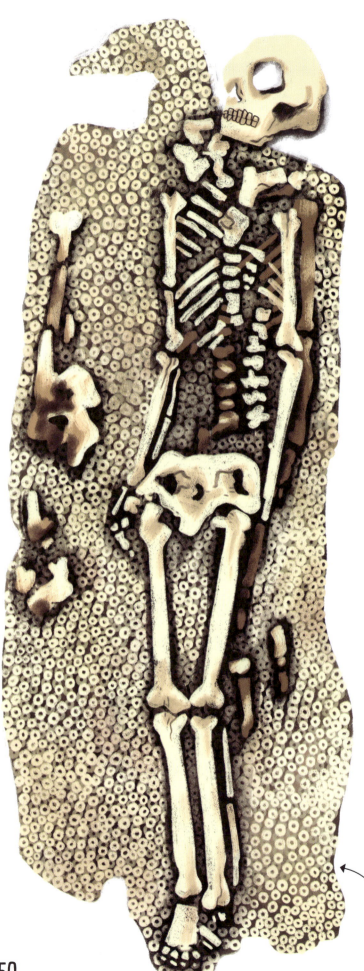

Melvin and his team started digging. As they reached the centre of the mound they found two burials, but there was something unusual about them – the two people were buried one on top of the other!

Nestled between the bodies were ancient Cahokian beads. Not just one or two, but 20,000! Melvin knew right away, whoever was buried here was extremely important. This wasn't the only thing that stood out though. The beads were arranged in the shape of a large falcon. The archaeologists dubbed it the **birdman burial**.

Melvin and his team then uncovered another pit that had been lined with large timbers. Inside, underneath 1,000 years of Mississippi mud, were the remains of 53 women. And that wasn't the only pit containing bodies – they found roughly 250 people buried alongside Mound 72.

All of this begs the question, who was in Mound 72 and why were there so many people next to them? Modern archaeology is uncovering some of the answers, but much remains shrouded by the mists of time.

Can you see the falcon shape?

The first clue is the age of Mound 72. Melvin was able to send some of the artefacts away to be dated. It seems the people were buried here around the year 1050 CE. That is hugely important because that was just after the founding of the city of Cahokia. Melvin may have uncovered the grave of **Cahokia's first ever rulers**. The people buried alongside them may have sacrificed themselves in honour of their city's founders, or maybe they were captors sacrificed against their will. We can't say for sure.

We're not even sure if the birdman... was even a man! Melvin presumed the bodies buried next to the bead bird cape were men, but modern archaeologists are questioning that assumption. Thomas Emerson, Kristin Hedman, and Eve Hargrave reanalysed the bones excavated by Melvin. And it seems he made a mistake: the birdman burial was not two men, but **a man and a woman**. Was this couple the original royal family of Cahokia? That's a mystery for future archaeologists to solve. Whoever they were, they were clearly respected enough that Cahokians for generations after would make sacrifices in their honour.

Birdman when he was alive

GLOSSARY

Ancestor

A family relative from a long time ago.

Aqueduct

A system invented for transporting water over large distances. The Romans were famous for their impressive aqueducts.

Archaeologist

Someone who studies the physical stuff humans make and leave behind. Archaeologists want to learn more about how humans lived in the past.

Archaeology

The study of all the physical stuff humans make and leave behind – including our bones.

Artefact

An object, usually made by humans, associated with an archaeological site.

BCE

Stands for "Before Common Era". It is used beside dates to differentiate them from years in the Common Era (*see* "CE"). For example: "Tutankhamun died in 1323 BCE".

The Bronze Age

A period in human history when humans started being able to shape metal (such as bronze) to make more useful tools, and the first cities appeared.

CE

Stands for "Common Era". The Common Era began in the year 0. It is used beside dates to differentiate them from years that occured before the Common Era (*see* "BCE"). For example: "The city of Pompeii was buried in 79 CE".

Celts

The inhabitants of areas of Western Europe roughly 2,000 years ago. Their culture lives on in many modern nations.

Coprolite

A fancy word for a fossilised poo! Coprolites are studied by scientists because they can tell us a lot about the diet of the person (or animal, or dinosaur) that was responsible for it.

Cuneiform

One of the earliest forms of writing. It first appeared in parts of Mesopotamia.

Drone

A flying machine. Drones are increasingly being used by archaeologists to study places that are hard to get to for people, or to look at the land from great heights.

Emperor

The ruler of an empire.

Empire

A collection of countries or territories ruled by one person – the emperor. Examples include the Roman Empire and the Inca Empire.

Evolution

The process by which different species change or adapt over time to better suit the environment they live in.

Extinct

Refers to a species of human, animal, or plant that has died out and no longer exists on Earth.

Fossil

A piece of living material, for example a bone or a leaf, that has turned into rock over millions of years underground. Fossils can tell us lots about what life was like in the past.

Geologist

Someone who studies rocks and the formation of the Earth.

Geology

The study of the rocks that make up the Earth.

Gladiator

A fighter, usually a slave, who fought other gladiators in stadiums for the entertainment of the people of ancient Rome.

Hieroglyphs

The system of writing, made up of lots of small pictures, that was used by the ancient Egyptians.

Homo sapiens

You, dear reader, are a Homo sapiens. It is the official name for our species of human. Other species of human include Neanderthals.

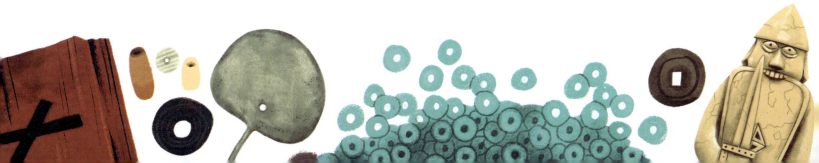

Ice age

A period when large parts of the Earth were covered in ice. There have been many ice ages. The last cold period ended around 11,000 years ago.

Maya

A group of people who originated in Central America. The Maya are famous for their incredible temples, calendars, and art.

Medieval period

A period of European history that took place from the 5th century to the 15th century. Also known as the Middle Ages. The Medieval period was a time of kings and queens, castles, and exploration.

Mesopotamia

An area in the Middle East that saw the rise of some of the first major civilisations, as well as the development of writing.

Midden

An archeological term for a pile of rubbish. But what might have been rubbish for one civilisation is invaluable to archaeologists studying it.

Minoans

People from a Bronze Age civilisation centred on the Greek island of Crete.

Mycenaeans

Ancient Greeks who lived in the years 1600 BCE to 1100 BCE.

Neanderthals

An extinct species of human who were shorter and stockier than Homo sapiens, but who shared many similarities in terms of intelligence and culture.

Nomad

Someone who doesn't live in one place, but moves around.

Pharaoh

The name for the kings of ancient Egypt.

Polynesians

People who live on islands in a region of the Pacific Ocean called Polynesia. Famously great sailors.

Prehistory

A very vague term that refers to the period of time before there were written records.

Samurai

The historical ruling warrior class of Japan.

Sarcophagus

A decorated stone coffin used by civilisations such as ancient Egypt.

Slave

Someone owned by another human and forced to do things against their own will.

Sonar

A scientific technique that fires sound waves underwater – and waits for them to bounce back – in order to find shipwrecks or hidden artefacts.

Stele

A piece of stone covered with an inscription. Often used as a monument by rulers in the ancient world.

Steppe

The grassy plains that make up parts of Europe and Asia. Historically the steppe was ruled by nomadic horse riders.

The Stone Age

A large period of prehistory where humans mostly used stone to make tools.

Tablet

A piece of clay that could be written on with a stick called a stylus, before being left to harden.

Tell

An archaeological term refering to a distinct mound or small hill that indicates humans have lived there in the past.

Trilithon

A structure formed of two vertical stones with a third stone laid horizontally over the top. Trilithons are found at prehistoric sites such as Stonehenge.

Vikings

Sea-faring people from Scandinavia who raided large parts of Europe between the years 700 CE and 1100 CE.

Ziggurat

A type of tower from ancient Mesopotamia formed of different levels that decreased in size until they reached the top.

INDEX

This has been a

NEON 🦑 SQUID

production

For Zoe

Author: Stefan Milosavljevich
Illustrator: Sam Caldwell
Consultant: Anna Goldfield

Neon Squid would like to thank:

Allison Singer for editing the American edition; Darren Parry for advising on the pages concerning Native American history; Jane Simmonds for proofreading; Elizabeth Wise for compiling the index; and Ella Walker for inspiring the book.

Copyright © 2022 St. Martin's Press
120 Broadway, New York, NY 10271

Created for St. Martin's Press by Neon Squid
The Stables, 4 Crinan Street, London, N1 9XW

EU representative: Macmillan
Publishers Ireland Ltd,
1st Floor, The Liffey Trust Centre, 117-126
Sheriff Street Upper, Dublin 1, D01 YC43

10 9 8 7 6 5 4 3 2

The right of Stefan Milosavljevich to be identified as the author of this work has been asserted in accordance with the Copyright, Designs and Patents Act, 1988.

A CIP catalogue record for this book is available from the British Library.

Printed and bound by Vivar Printing in Malaysia.

ISBN: 978-1-83899-156-2

www.neonsquidbooks.com